TEACHER'S RESOURCE MANUAL

GLOBE FEARON

ENGLISH

at School and on the Job

Upper Saddle River, New Jersey
www.globefearon.com

Content Reviewer: Wendy Gdanski, English Teacher
DeWitt-Clinton High School
Bronx, New York

Supervising Editor: Lynn W. Kloss
Component Editor: Monica Glina
Editor: Kevin Iwano
Editorial Assistant: Dara Eisenstein
Production Editor: Marcela Maslanczuk
Senior Designer: Janice Noto-Helmers
Designer: Sharon Scannell
Illustrator: John Bleck
Composition and Layout: Mimi Raihl, Susan Levine, Wanda Rockwell, Jeffrey Engel
Manufacturing Supervisor: Mark Cirillo

Photo Credits: p. 3 David Young-Wolff, Photo Edit; p. 9 Michael Newman, Photo Edit;
p. 16 Bonnie Kamin, Photo Edit; p. 26 Michael Newman, Photo Edit;
p. 35 Myrleen Ferguson, Photo Edit; p. 46 David Young-Wolff, Photo Edit;
p. 52 Spencer Grant, Photo Edit; p. 63 Michael Newman, Photo Edit;
p. 74 David Young-Wolff, Photo Edit; p. 87 Bill Aron, Photo Edit;
p. 96 Spencer Grant, Photo Edit; p. 106 Bill Aron, Photo Edit;
p. 119 John Neubauer, Photo Edit; p. 127 Myrleen Ferguson, Photo Edit

Printed in the United States of America   2 3 4 5 6 7 8 9 10   05 04 03 02 01 00

ISBN: 0-130-23263-7

1-800-848-9500
www.globefearon.com

CONTENTS

The Student Edition builds skills for listening, speaking, reading, and writing.

Globe Fearon English at School and on the Job is a fully integrated program that includes grammar, mechanics, and usage instruction; critical-thinking activities; real-life writing samples; career case studies; technology connections; and portfolio projects.

Learning Objectives help students preview the key concepts and skills they will learn in each chapter.

Key Words help students grasp the lesson topics.

CHAPTER **4**

BEGINNING THE WRITING PROCESS

Kai has been accepted into a trainee program in the store in which she works. If she does well, she will quickly advance in the company. As a management trainee, Kai is asked to write about herself and her goals. She is unsure of what to write. She does not know which details to include and which ones to leave out. Although Kai knows what her goals are, she does not know how to express them clearly in her writing.

Key Words

process

purpose

audience

chronological order

sequence

spatial order

comparison

contrast

Goals for Success

In this chapter, you will learn these skills:

Deciding how to write for specific purposes and audiences

SCANS PROBLEM-SOLVING

Choosing and narrowing writing topics

SCANS ACQUIRING AND EVALUATING INFORMATION

Collecting information to use in writing

SCANS MATERIALS AND FACILITIES

Using graphic organizers to assemble ideas as preparation for writing

SCANS ORGANIZING AND MAINTAINING INFORMATION

Creating a word-processing document

SCANS USING COMPUTERS TO PROCESS INFORMATION

PORTFOLIO PROJECT

WRITING ABOUT GOALS

By the time you complete this chapter, you will know what Kai has to do to write about her goals. You also will be able to write about your own career goals and add your work to your portfolio.

Case Studies feature realistic workplace scenarios your students can relate to.

Portfolio Projects relate students' writing to their career development.

SCANS skills, which are correlated to the chapter objectives, demonstrate the integration of workplace skills and competencies.

What Do You Already Know? activates students' prior knowledge to set the stage for learning.

Introductory paragraphs answer the question "Why should I learn this?"

Workplace documents offer models of effective writing.

Check Your Understanding questions help students review the lesson topic.

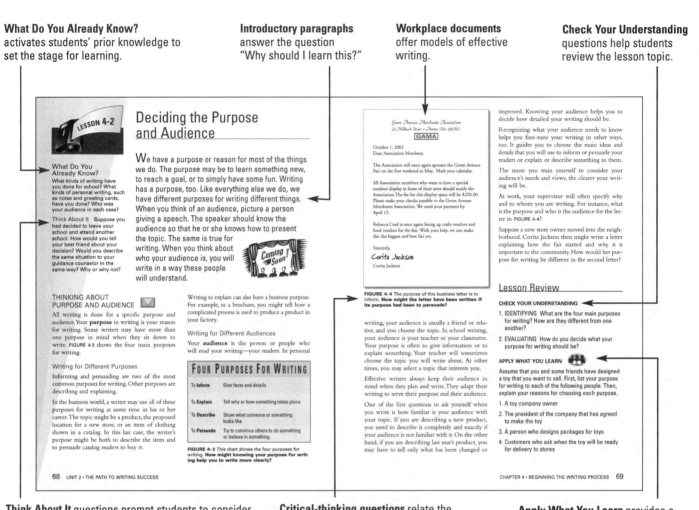

Think About It questions prompt students to consider how the topic connects to their daily lives.

Critical-thinking questions relate the visuals to the skills taught in each lesson.

Apply What You Learn provides a real-life application of learning.

Grammar Workshops help students develop essential grammar skills in the context of the workplace.

Handbook references at point of use direct students to a complete in-text resource that reinforces reading, writing, grammar, and mechanics skills and strategies.

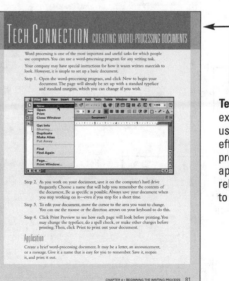

Tech Connections explain how to use technology effectively, provide hands-on applications, and relate technology to the workplace.

The Teacher's Resource Manual offers ideas to reinforce, extend, and customize instruction.

This valuable resource includes comprehensive lesson support and options to reinforce or extend the lesson.

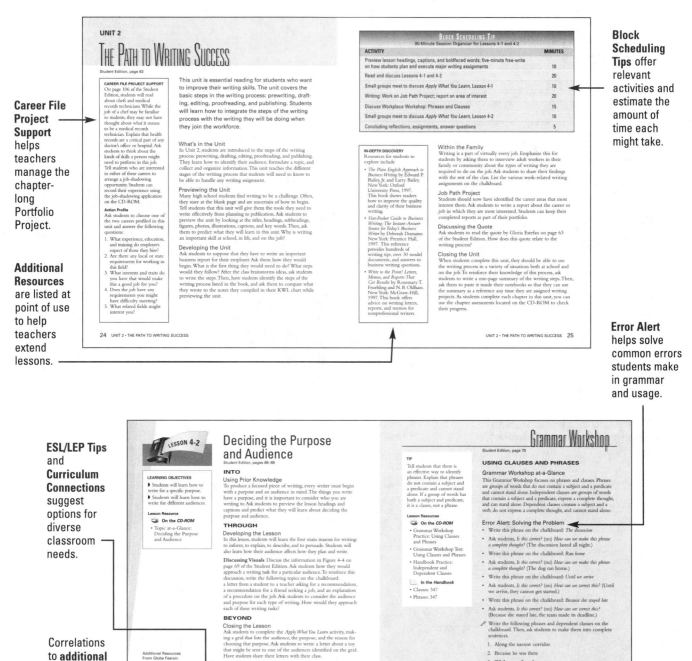

Career File Project Support helps teachers manage the chapter-long Portfolio Project.

Additional Resources are listed at point of use to help teachers extend lessons.

ESL/LEP Tips and **Curriculum Connections** suggest options for diverse classroom needs.

Correlations to **additional Globe Fearon products** can be used to extend instruction.

Block Scheduling Tips offer relevant activities and estimate the amount of time each might take.

Error Alert helps solve common errors students make in grammar and usage.

The Teacher's Resource CD-ROM maximizes teaching support with a wealth of options.

The searchable Teacher's Resource CD-ROM includes reproducible activity sheets that teachers can use or customize.

Features of the Teacher's Resource CD-ROM:

... that can

- ... Workshop for ... and assessment

- Activities ... topic

- Graphic organizers that help students organize information before writing

- Sample résumés, business letters, and other examples of business writing

- Topics-at-a-glance that reinforce subject matter

- Applications that offer students practice and reinforcement of what they have learned

---

THESE ADDITIONAL RESOURCES FROM GLOBE FEARON CAN HELP EXTEND LESSONS.

Writer's Toolkit CD-ROM On this interactive CD-ROM, students can use more than 50 tools and activities to learn the skills and the process of writing. (Interest levels 6–12)

Be a Better Reader This flexible reading program increases students' reading skills and enhances their comprehension in the four major content areas. (Reading levels 4–10, Interest levels 6–12)

Reading in the Content Areas This reading program teaches students how to navigate and comprehend nonfiction text in the four content areas by using a selection of reading strategies. (Reading levels 4–7, Interest levels 6–12)

Globe Fearon English Exercise Books This series offers students a wealth of practice opportunities to master basic English skills: paragraphs, sentences, parts of speech, mechanics and usage, punctuation, and vocabulary. (Reading levels 6–8, Interest levels 6–12)

Success in Writing This series offers instruction in the four modes of writing: description, explanation, persuasion, and narration. It also teaches grammar in the context of writing. (Reading level 5, Interest levels 6–12)

Language Arts Skills Chart

SKILLS	STUDENT EDITION CHAPTERS													
	1	2	3	4	5	6	7	8	9	10	11	12	13	14
1. Write for a variety of purposes, such as personal, business, explanatory, informative, persuasive, and narrative	✓	✓	✓	✓	✓	✓	✓	✓	✓	✓	✓	✓	✓	✓
2. Write on a variety of tasks and for many different audiences	✓	✓	✓	✓	✓	✓	✓	✓	✓	✓	✓	✓	✓	✓
3. Generate, draft, evaluate, revise, and edit ideas in writing	✓	✓	✓	✓	✓	✓	✓	✓	✓	✓	✓	✓	✓	✓
4. Develop effective choices in the organization of writing, including details and appropriate conventions of written English	✓	✓		✓	✓			✓						✓
5. Write in a voice and style appropriate to the audience and purpose			✓	✓	✓									
6. Organize ideas in writing to ensure coherence, logical progression, and support for ideas	✓	✓	✓	✓	✓									
7. Select and use appropriate strategies to generate ideas, develop voice, and plan an argument		✓		✓										
8. Develop drafts by organizing content and by refining style to suit audience and purpose		✓		✓	✓									
9. Proofread writing for appropriateness of organization, content, style, and conventions	✓	✓	✓	✓	✓	✓	✓	✓	✓	✓	✓	✓	✓	✓
10. Publish finished pieces of writing	✓	✓	✓	✓	✓	✓	✓	✓	✓	✓	✓	✓	✓	✓
11. Select and use appropriate prewriting strategies	✓	✓		✓										
12. Write drafts that are focused, purposeful, and organized	✓	✓			✓									
13. Produce error-free writing in the final draft		✓			✓				✓	✓	✓	✓		
14. Write a report using formal or informal research								✓						
15. Write to effectively communicate ideas and information	✓	✓	✓	✓	✓	✓	✓	✓	✓	✓	✓	✓	✓	✓
16. Write for real or potentially real situations in academic, professional, and civic contexts	✓	✓	✓	✓	✓	✓	✓	✓	✓	✓	✓	✓	✓	✓

SKILLS	STUDENT EDITION CHAPTERS													
	1	2	3	4	5	6	7	8	9	10	11	12	13	14
17. Select and use a variety of electronic media, such as the Internet, e-mail, interactive video, CD-ROM, information services, and desktop publishing systems	✓	✓	✓	✓	✓	✓	✓	✓	✓	✓	✓	✓	✓	✓
18. Compile information from primary and secondary sources in systematic ways using available technology	✓	✓	✓	✓			✓	✓	✓		✓	✓	✓	
19. Represent information in a variety of ways, such as graphics, conceptual maps, and learning logs	✓		✓	✓			✓	✓	✓	✓	✓	✓		✓
20. Compile written ideas and representations into reports, summaries, or other formats and draw conclusions	✓		✓	✓		✓	✓	✓	✓	✓	✓	✓	✓	✓
21. Evaluate his or her own writing and the writing of others	✓	✓			✓	✓	✓	✓	✓	✓	✓	✓	✓	✓
22. Evaluate writing for both mechanics and content	✓	✓	✓	✓	✓	✓	✓	✓	✓	✓	✓	✓	✓	✓
23. Respond productively to peer review of his/her own work		✓			✓	✓	✓	✓						
24. Select and use appropriate listening strategies according to the intended purpose	✓	✓	✓	✓	✓	✓	✓	✓	✓	✓	✓	✓	✓	✓
25. Select and use a variety of speaking strategies to clarify meaning and to reflect understanding and application of content	✓	✓	✓	✓	✓	✓	✓	✓	✓	✓	✓	✓	✓	✓
26. Use details, illustrations, analogies, and visual aids to make oral presentations that inform, persuade, or entertain			✓				✓				✓	✓	✓	✓
27. Apply oral communication skills to interviews, presentations, and impromptu situations	✓	✓	✓	✓			✓		✓		✓	✓	✓	✓
28. Integrate multimedia and technologies into presentations			✓						✓		✓			✓
29. Become lifelong independent learners and continue to grow in the ability to communicate	✓	✓	✓	✓	✓	✓	✓	✓	✓	✓	✓	✓	✓	✓
30. Use spoken, written, and visual language to accomplish specific purposes, such as learning, enjoyment, persuasion, and the exchange of information	✓	✓	✓	✓	✓	✓	✓	✓	✓	✓	✓	✓	✓	✓

TO THE TEACHER

Globe Fearon English at School and on the Job offers a practical, comprehensive approach to success in English. Students learn writing, reading, speaking, and listening skills, as well as the grammatical and technical aspects of writing that are critical at school and on the job. *English at School and on the Job* introduces these topics in a thoughtful, engaging way that demonstrates to students the practical importance of key communication skills.

The REACT strategy incorporates five essential forms of learning—Relating, Experiencing, Applying, Cooperating, and Transferring—that are emphasized in *English at School and on the Job*. REACT is based on the concept that students learn most successfully when they have the chance to relate what they are learning to their own needs and interests. *English at School and on the Job* gives students the chance to Relate what they are learning to experiences they have already had through focused activities. Students get practical Experience writing documents, such as résumés and cover letters. Students Apply what they learn in projects ranging from investigating careers to preparing a presentation. Every chapter has opportunities for students to practice Cooperative learning to achieve results. Finally, students learn to Transfer their skills to new situations. For example, a student who feels confident writing a personal letter can move on to writing many kinds of business letters.

English at School and on the Job is an integrated program that provides an array of resources focused on teaching English. This Teacher's Resource Manual offers comprehensive lesson support, lesson planning guides, and a complete answer key. The Teacher's Resource CD-ROM provides lesson reinforcement and assessment opportunities. Additional resources from Globe Fearon, such as *Be a Better Reader, Reading in the Content Areas, Writer's Toolkit, Globe Exercise Books,* and *Success in Writing* are all referenced for easy integration into this program.

Using This Book

The Teacher's Resource Manual offers both specific ideas for teaching the material in *English at School and on the Job* and suggestions for expanding student and class involvement.

- Each Unit Opener offers ideas for introducing, previewing, and developing the unit. The opener also offers suggestions for books that students might want to use for further study, a discussion of the quote that appears in each unit, and block scheduling tips.

- Each Chapter Opener introduces the scenario that begins every chapter. It provides suggestions for how to teach the Portfolio Project that appears at the end of each chapter. The Chapter Opener discusses the specific CD-ROM Teamwork/Cooperative activity that can be used with the chapter.

- Each lesson plan contains the following parts:

  INTO: **Using Prior Knowledge** uses students' personal experiences to engage them.

  THROUGH: **Developing the Lesson** summarizes the lesson's content and addresses important visuals or checklists presented in the Student Edition.

  BEYOND: **Closing the Lesson** contains suggestions for expanding the Apply What You Learn activity that appears at the end of each lesson in the Student Edition. While the Beyond section always contains Closing the Lesson, it also features different elements that allow you to continue to challenge students. The Beyond categories include ESL/LEP Tip, Extending the Lesson, Curriculum Connection, Web Activity, and Job Path Project.

Special Features

THE JOB PATH PROJECT

The Job Path Project is a year-long, student-directed investigation of careers. Students first explore careers and then choose one on which to focus. As the year progresses, students create résumés and cover letters designed for that career; interview someone in their field of choice; arrange a job-shadowing experience; and prepare and deliver a report that focuses on their field. This project sharpens students' understanding of the steps involved in a job search and helps them begin a serious exploration of their field of choice.

GRAMMAR WORKSHOPS

These pages provide ideas to help students overcome specific errors that often occur with certain grammatical topics. Students are given specific examples that contain errors and are asked to resolve the errors. Each Grammar Workshop ends with an exercise that tests students' skills.

TECH CONNECTIONS

The Tech Connections that appear at the end of each chapter in the Student Edition are discussed at the end of each unit in this Teacher's Resource Manual. Activities help students understand the practical relevance of each Tech Connection topic introduced in the Student Edition.

Strategies for Teaching the Key Words

The vocabulary words highlighted in each chapter were chosen for their relevance to the worlds of school and of business. While the Student Edition defines words in context, there are several ways to approach *teaching* the key words:

- Teach the words, which appear in boldface type, as they are introduced in the chapter.
- Show students how to use context clues to decode the meaning. Context clues, such as restating a word's meaning, finding a word that is its opposite within the sentence, or looking for clues within surrounding words and phrases, are ways that help students understand unfamiliar words.
- Show students how to decode words using prefixes, suffixes, and words within a family.
- Ask students to keep a personal dictionary. Students should be listing, defining, and using the highlighted vocabulary words in sentences.

Strategies for Teaching ESL/LEP Students

Students learning English face particular challenges at school and in the workplace. The business world utilizes terms and words that are often not taught in conventional English classes. There are several techniques that can help students learning English:

- Ask English-proficient students to read aloud. Hearing the language makes it easier to grasp meaning through emphasis and intonation.
- Ask students to keep a running list of unfamiliar words and expressions that you or another student can define for them.
- If possible, pair an English-proficient student with a less proficient one. Both students can gain a deeper understanding of language by analyzing it in detail together.
- Emphasize postreading activities that are visual, written, and oral so that students can gain information in various ways.
- Reinforce your teaching by repeating and rephrasing information, using synonyms, and employing body language. These techniques offer students a variety of ways to understand the assignment.
- Ask students to provide a written summary of what they have read. This technique is useful for judging whether students understand the main point of a section or chapter. Use the completed assignment as a model that students can refer to.
- Encourage students to ask for help or clarification of any concepts or directions that are unclear. Remember that in some cultures, students who do not understand directions are not encouraged to ask questions.
- Encourage students to write, even though they will make errors. At first, emphasize general content over mechanics.
- Involve students in group activities by making sure students are in a group that can provide them with help and to which they can contribute.
- Remind students that they have unique experiences that can benefit the entire class. Encourage them to share these experiences with their classmates.

 ## Using the CD-ROM

The CD-ROM component of *Globe Fearon English at School and on the Job* is a digital Classroom Resource Binder that can be invaluable in helping students polish and practice their skills. Each element of the CD-ROM is tied closely to the Student Edition and is designed to enrich and extend the key concepts and skills presented there. By providing additional instruction, worksheets, and activities to supplement the lessons in the Student Edition, the CD-ROM further emphasizes English in the context of school and the workplace. This CD-ROM allows you not only to print the materials from it, but to edit them as well. Due to this flexibility, the files allow you to customize materials required for the needs of individual students or classes. It also allows you to assemble tests using questions from different files.

UNIT 1

YOU AND YOUR CAREER

Student Edition, page 1

On page 62 of the Student Edition, students will read

CAREER FILE PROJECT SUPPORT
On page 62 of the Student Edition, students will read about landscapers and radiologic technologists. Review the descriptions for each of these with students. Explain to students that one of the hurdles of career planning is understanding exactly what people in different jobs do. What kinds of skills does each of these jobs require? Talk about what personal traits would lead to success in these fields.

Action Profile
Ask students to choose one of the two careers profiled in this unit and answer the following questions:

1. What experience, education, and training do employers expect of those they hire?
2. Are there any local or state requirements for working in this field?
3. What interests and traits do you have that would make this a good job for you?
4. Does the job have any requirements you might have difficulty meeting?
5. What related fields might interest you?

By the end of this unit, your students will have thought about the types of careers that intrigue them. Once they have identified a field of choice, they will have learned how to research specific jobs that interest them. Students will have learned how to present themselves on paper and in person, how to get the position they are pursuing, and how to become a valuable member of any team.

What is in the Unit

Unit 1 focuses on the path from school to career. First, students explore their career goals. They assess their interests and personality traits and learn key workplace skills. Then, they learn how to search for a job. They learn how to write résumés and cover letters, how to prepare for job interviews, and how to evaluate their interviews. Finally, students learn how to become valuable members of a team by making effective decisions, resolving conflicts, organizing their work, and prioritizing their tasks.

Previewing the Unit

Most students enjoy thinking about life after high school. Ask students to preview the unit by looking at the titles, headings, subheadings, figures, photos, illustrations, captions, key words, sample letters, and résumés. Then, ask them to predict what they will learn in this unit. Encourage students to discuss jobs they have already had. How did they get their job? How might their job after high school be different?

Developing the Unit

Ask students to describe a career they would like to pursue by writing a short description of that career and the steps they would take to get it. Encourage students to think about the kinds of interests and traits a person in such a position might possess. Are these interests and traits similar to their own?

ACTIVITY	MINUTES
Preview lesson headings, captions, and boldface words; five-minute free-write on careers students might choose and why	10
Read and discuss Lessons 1-1 and 1-2	20
Writing: Students work on self-assessment log	20
Small groups meet to work on *Apply What You Learn*, Lesson 1-1	10
Discuss Grammar Workshop: Writing Complete Sentences	15
Small groups meet to discuss *Apply What You Learn*, Lesson 1-2	10
Concluding reflections; assignments; answer questions	5

IN-DEPTH DISCOVERY

Resources for students to explore include

- *Career Exploration on the Internet: A Student's Guide to More Than 300 Web Sites!* edited by Elizabeth H. Oakes, Chicago, IL: Ferguson Publishing, 1998. This book summarizes the main career Web sites and provides new ideas and leads for job seekers.

- *Job Hunting in the 21st Century: Exploding the Myths, Exploring the Realities* by Carol A. Hacker, Boca Raton, FL: CRC Press— St. Lucie Press, 1999. This book discusses salary and benefits negotiation. It also includes job interview practice questions.

- *What Color Is Your Parachute? 2000* by Richard Nelson Bolles, Berkeley, CA: Ten Speed Press, 1999. This is a manual for job hunters and a guide for career changers.

Within the Community

Ask students what careers they might like to pursue. Then, arrange classroom visits from members of the community who work in some of these fields. Ask students to prepare a list of questions for each guest speaker. They might ask what kinds of skills and qualities are useful in those fields and if any job-shadowing or internship opportunities are available.

Job Path Project

The Job Path Project is a Teacher's Resource Manual activity designed to help students identify and explore a potential career. The Job Path activities in this unit help students choose a potential career, create a career plan, write a résumé and a cover letter, and prepare for a job interview. You might consider distributing a career plan and sample résumés and cover letters that can be found on the CD-ROM. Ask students to keep the information they gather for the Job Path Project in their portfolios.

Discussing the Quote

Ask students to read the quote by Michael Jordan on page 1 of the Student Edition. How does this quote relate to searching for a job and preparing for an interview?

Closing the Unit

After completing this unit, students should be actively thinking about their work lives after high school. Wrap up the unit with a five-minute session in which students identify the most important job skills they learned. Emphasize that the next units will help students learn the writing skills they will need to be successful on the job. As your students complete each chapter in this unit, you can use the chapter assessments located on the CD-ROM to check their progress.

Student Edition, pages 2–3

YOUR CAREER GOALS
English in Context

TEACHING THE CHAPTER OPENER

Many students can probably identify with Charles's difficulties setting career goals. Charles has found jobs and has been successful at them, but he has not thought about his long-term plans. Use Charles's experience to discuss how and why young people should create a career plan.

• Ask your students to suppose that they are career counselors. What steps would they suggest Charles take when thinking about his future?

PORTFOLIO SETUP: WRITING A CAREER PLAN

• On page 19 of the Student Edition, students are asked to write a career plan. Ask students to do a ten-minute writing exercise in which they identify a job that interests them. What kinds of skills or training would they need for that job? You might consider asking students to use Creating a Career Plan on the CD-ROM. Ask students to place their completed work in their portfolio.

CD-ROM TEAMWORK/COOPERATIVE ACTIVITY

• The CD-ROM has suggestions for setting up a job-shadowing program. Students can use the information they received from the guest speakers in the Within the Community activity on page 2 of this Teacher's Resource Manual. Each program participant is assigned one of the tasks, which include Internet research, employer recruiter, student publicist, and teacher-student liaison. The activity includes a schedule that can be used to show the different tasks and the order in which to do them.

LESSON PLANNING CHART

CHAPTER 1	STUDENT EDITION PAGES	TEACHER'S RESOURCE MANUAL PAGES	CD-ROM
Writing/Reading Activities	7, 8, 11, 16–19	3, 5, 6, 8	✓
Speaking/Listening Activities	13, 16, 19	4, 6, 7	✓
Career Activities	7, 11, 13, 16, 19	3, 8	✓
Critical Thinking Activities	4, 7, 9, 12, 14, 18, 19	3, 4, 6–8	✓
Vocabulary Activities	3, 18		✓
ESL/LEP Tips		4, 6, 7	
Teamwork/Cooperative Activities	16, 19	3, 7	✓
Curriculum Connections		4	
Technology Activities	17	8, 23	✓

LEARNING OBJECTIVE

▶ Students will learn how to assess work-related skills.

Assessing Your Skills
Student Edition, pages 4–7

INTO

Using Prior Knowledge

Many of your students have probably held part-time or summer jobs. Ask students what skills helped them to succeed in these jobs. List their answers on the chalkboard. Encourage students to discuss the job requirements that surprised them. These could include their employers' insistence on a suitable appearance or on promptness. Then, ask students to preview the lesson headings and captions and predict what they will learn about assessing their skills.

THROUGH

Developing the Lesson

This lesson discusses how to plan for a career. Students learn how to consider job trends, how to complete a self-assessment log to pinpoint their skills and interests, and how these might translate into a career. The lesson also includes a list of entry-level workplace skills.

Discussing Visuals Emphasize workplace skills by reviewing Figure 1-2 on page 6 of the Student Edition. Read each key workplace skill aloud. Then, ask students to describe what they would do in each situation. You could also have small groups develop responses to each situation, and then ask the groups to share their responses with the class.

BEYOND

Closing the Lesson

After students finish rating themselves in the *Apply What You Learn* activity, ask them to form groups to discuss the results. In which area did they rate average or superior? Which areas require improvement? How can these skills be developed or refined?

ESL/LEP Tip

Suggest that students create a Career Word list. They can begin with the definitions of career-related words and phrases such as *customer, co-worker, boss, employee, supervisor,* and *foreman.* Ask students to use each word in an original sentence.

Curriculum Connection: Science

Workplace safety is one focus of the entry-level workplace skills in this lesson. Students may want to explore the role and influence of the Occupational Safety and Health Administration (OSHA) in the United States. Why are OSHA's workplace rules and regulations important? Students can use reference sources, such as newspapers and online search engines, in their research.

TIP

Explain to students that even imperative sentences with only one word—such as "Stop!" and "Go!"—have a subject. The subject is not stated, but it is understood to be *you*.

Lesson Resources

On the *CD-ROM*

- Grammar Workshop Practice: Writing Complete Sentences
- Grammar Workshop Test: Writing Complete Sentences

In the *Handbook*

- Sentences: 346

Additional Resources From Globe Fearon:

- *Globe Exercise Book*
  Sentences: 6–7

- *Success in Writing*
  Grammar Skills for Writers: 9, 10

- *Writer's Toolkit*
  Handbook: Grammar Handbook: The Sentence and Its Parts

WRITING COMPLETE SENTENCES

Grammar Workshop at-a-Glance

In this Grammar Workshop, students focus on what is and is not a sentence. They identify sentence fragments and learn how to create sentences using them.

Error Alert: Solving the Problem

- Write this fragment on the chalkboard: *finished the report*

- Ask students, *Does this sound correct?* (No; it needs a subject.)

- Ask students, *How can we correct this fragment so that it is a complete sentence?* (We finished the report.)

- Write this fragment on the chalkboard: *wrote his recommendation*

- Ask students, *Does this sound correct?* (No; it needs a subject.)

- Ask students, *How can we correct this fragment so that it is a complete sentence?* (He wrote his recommendation.)

- Write this fragment on the chalkboard: *you the job*

- Ask students, *Does this sound correct?* (No; it needs a verb.)

- Ask students, *How can we correct this fragment so that it is a complete sentence?* (You got the job.)

- Write this fragment on the chalkboard: *we the conference*

- Ask students, *Does this sound correct?* (No; it needs a verb.)

- Ask students, *How can we correct this fragment so that it is a complete sentence?* (We attended the conference.)

Write the following sentences on the chalkboard. Ask students to rewrite each sentence fragment so that it is a complete sentence.

1. Receives the shipments (subject: Carla)

2. He a new employee (verb: hired)

3. Margaux the training session (verb: attended)

4. Complimented the team on its work (subject: The president)

5. Created an efficient system (subject: She)

Building Self-Confidence
Student Edition, pages 9–11

LEARNING OBJECTIVES

▶ Students will understand the relationship between self-confidence and success.

▶ Students will learn techniques to bolster their self-esteem.

Lesson Resource

On the *CD-ROM*

• Topic at-a-Glance: Creating a Career Plan

INTO

Using Prior Knowledge

How can you tell when someone is self-confident? How can you tell when someone lacks self-confidence? Ask students to brainstorm the answers to these questions. Then, ask them to draft a quick assessment of their own self-confidence. Ask students to preview the lesson headings and captions and predict what they will learn about building self-confidence.

THROUGH

Developing the Lesson

The lesson focuses on creating self-esteem and self-confidence, setting reasonable goals, asking for help, and celebrating success.

Discussing Visuals Review Figure 1-3, *Writing in the Real World: Career Plan*, on page 10 of the Student Edition. Ask students to reproduce the chart in Figure 1-3 and complete it. What is their long-term goal? What are their short-term goals? What target dates did they set for their short-term goals?

BEYOND

Closing the Lesson

Ask students to refer to their list of strengths from the *Apply What You Learn* activity. Ask students to think about skills they have that require improvement. How can they develop that strength?

ESL/LEP Tip

The words *self-esteem* and *self-confidence* have subtly different meanings. Make sure students learning English recognize that *self-confidence* refers to *confidence in one's abilities*, whereas *self-esteem* means *believing in oneself*. Ask students to add these terms and their definitions to their Career Word lists.

Extending the Lesson

Body language can be a powerful signal to others about how we feel. Ask students to look through magazines and newspapers and find examples of body language that illustrate low or high self-esteem. Ask students to describe what the body language tells them about the person in the photograph.

Developing Effective Work Habits

Student Edition, pages 12–13

LEARNING OBJECTIVE

▶ Students will learn to recognize effective work habits and how to achieve them.

INTO

Using Prior Knowledge

Ask students who have had jobs to talk about their work experiences. What examples can they give of good work habits? of work habits that need improvement? What difference do good work habits make in the workplace? Ask students to preview the lesson headings and captions and predict what they will learn about developing effective work habits.

THROUGH

Developing the Lesson

This lesson focuses on workplace behavior. It discusses being enthusiastic, being a self-starter, presenting a good image, making one's best effort, accepting criticism thoughtfully, and staying alert. Discuss each one of these work habits with your students. Ask a volunteer to give either an example from a work experience or create an example for each main point. How are these work habits referred to in classified advertisements?

BEYOND

Closing the Lesson

Ask students to compile the results of their interviews from the *Apply What You Learn* activity. Have them form groups and discuss the results. What advice was cited most frequently? What makes the advice so valuable?

ESL/LEP Tip

Understanding a country's cultural mores and signals is as challenging as learning the language. For example, what a North American might consider enthusiastic, a resident of another continent might consider nosy. Ask students if the effective workplace behaviors discussed on pages 12 and 13 of the Student Edition are appropriate behaviors in their countries. What are considered effective workplace habits in their countries?

Extending the Lesson

Ask students to role-play the different workplace behaviors discussed on pages 12 and 13 of the Student Edition. Tell students to pay attention to the kinds of reactions certain behaviors cause. How can a colleague's reaction to a student's behavior help to refine his or her workplace behavior?

Making Job Choices

Student Edition, pages 14–16

LEARNING OBJECTIVE

▶ Students will create and assess the stages of a job search.

Lesson Resources

On the *CD-ROM*

• Topic at-a-Glance: Using the Internet to Search for a Job

• Topic at-a-Glance: Job Shadowing

• Teamwork/Cooperative Activity: Setting up a Job-shadowing Program

INTO

Using Prior Knowledge

Ask students to share their earliest career aspirations. How have they changed? What careers currently interest them? How can they learn more about those careers? Ask students to preview the lesson headings and captions and predict what they will learn about making job choices.

THROUGH

Developing the Lesson

This lesson explains how to research a job by consulting printed materials. It also explains how to search for a job by networking, using employment offices, and exploring online information sources. Students also learn how entry-level jobs can provide the training necessary for future careers. Finally, students learn the importance of making a commitment to themselves by setting reasonable goals, maintaining good work habits, and rewarding themselves for a job well done.

BEYOND

Closing the Lesson

Ask students to respond to the research they did in the *Apply What You Learn* activity. Was the *Occupational Outlook Handbook* easy to find? Did it have a lot of useful information? Did the information about the necessary training and the salary surprise them?

Job Path Project

This lesson is the beginning of the Job Path Project, which allows students to explore a career in depth. (See the Unit Opener on page 2 of this Teacher's Resource Manual for more information.) Ask students to select a career that they would like to investigate further. The Job Path Project, which occurs throughout the Teacher's Resource Manual, will provide activities that will help students research, in depth, the careers they choose.

Web Activity

Ask students to search the Internet for the *Occupational Outlook Handbook* (stats.bls.gov/ocohome.htm). Then, ask them to use the *Handbook* to identify the careers that they would like to explore in the Job Path Project. Explain to students that this is their opportunity to choose a career that looks interesting and that they want to find out more about.

Student Edition, pages 20–21

FINDING THE RIGHT JOB

English in Context

TEACHING THE CHAPTER OPENER

Beth is a young woman who is good at her job and is anxious to advance. Unfortunately, there are no opportunities for advancement at the motel. Her goal is to work at a big hotel, but she does not know what steps to take in order to get that job.

• Discuss Beth's situation with the class. What steps should Beth take toward her goal? How can writing skills help Beth reach her goal?

PORTFOLIO SETUP: WRITING A COVER LETTER

• On page 41 of the Student Edition, students are asked to write a cover letter. The Job Path Project in Lesson 2-2 on page 11 of this Teacher's Resource Manual asks students to write résumés for a job in their chosen fields. Build on this work by asking students to write a cover letter to accompany each résumé. Ask students to write their cover letters based on classified ads they find in the newspaper or on the Internet.

CD-ROM TEAMWORK/COOPERATIVE ACTIVITY

• This activity helps create a support group for students who are searching for part-time work. Each student is assigned a task, such as searching for possible jobs or creating copies of résumés. Suggest that students who are actively looking for jobs form such a group and write a weekly report that details what the group has accomplished.

LESSON PLANNING CHART			
CHAPTER 2	STUDENT EDITION PAGES	TEACHER'S RESOURCE MANUAL PAGES	CD-ROM
Writing/Reading Activities	27, 31, 32, 40, 41	9–15	✓
Speaking/Listening Activities	23, 27, 31, 35, 38	9, 11, 12, 15	✓
Career Activities	22–24, 27, 28, 31, 33, 35, 36, 38–41	9–12, 15	✓
Critical Thinking Activities	22, 24, 28, 33, 36	9, 10, 12, 14, 15	✓
Vocabulary Activities	21, 40		✓
ESL/LEP Tips		12, 14	
Teamwork/Cooperative Activities	27, 31, 35, 38	9, 11, 12	✓
Curriculum Connections		11	
Technology Activities	39	10, 23	

Evaluating Job Opportunities

Student Edition, pages 22–23

LEARNING OBJECTIVE

▶ Students will learn how to search for and evaluate job opportunities.

INTO

Using Prior Knowledge

How have your students found jobs in the past? Explain to students that these can be volunteer jobs or jobs they were paid for. Which job search methods were most successful? List the methods students have used on the chalkboard. Then, ask students to preview the lesson headings and captions and predict what they will learn about evaluating job opportunities.

THROUGH

Developing the Lesson

Identifying job opportunities, searching for these opportunities, and keeping track of the job hunt with a job log are the main topics of this lesson. Students learn that a job hunt should be an active process.

Discussing Visuals Discuss Figure 2-1 on page 23 of the Student Edition. Discuss the ways in which a job log can be useful. How does a job log help students keep track of tasks?

BEYOND

Closing the Lesson

After students do their interviews for the *Apply What You Learn* activity, ask them to share the advice they were given. Record this advice on the chalkboard. What pieces of advice were cited most frequently? Why? How can students use the advice to advance their own job searches?

Job Path Project

Ask students to remind themselves of their long- and short-term career goals. Where will they begin their job search? Do they have any contacts in that industry? Under what categories do their jobs appear in the Classified Ads section of the newspaper? Then, ask students to create a job log that contains leads for jobs. Encourage students to use their logs during the job-search process.

Web Activity

Students can expand upon the research they did in the *Apply What You Learn* activity by researching the various employment Web sites available on the Internet. Ask students to visit www.monster.com or www.jobfind.com. Then, ask them to search for jobs in the careers they chose for the Job Path Project. What kinds of information were they able to find on these sites? What makes these sites useful resources for job searching?

Writing a Résumé
Student Edition, pages 24–27

INTO

Using Prior Knowledge

A résumé is a summary of a person's employment history, skills, and qualifications. Ask students why a résumé might be necessary. What kind of information is an employer looking for? Then, ask students to preview the lesson headings and captions and predict what they will learn about writing a résumé.

THROUGH

Developing the Lesson

Students learn the purpose of a résumé. They learn the types of information that a résumé should include and are given a list of information that will help make their résumés complete. Students then learn how to write a first draft. They learn that a résumé should fit on one business-letter page. They also learn to use a font that is easy to read and to print their résumés on white paper.

Discussing Visuals Review Figure 2-2, *Writing in the Real World: Résumé*, on page 25 of the Student Edition with your students. Ask students to suppose that they are prospective employers. What did they learn about Melody from her résumé?

BEYOND

Closing the Lesson

Use the *Apply What You Learn* activity as an editing workshop. Ask pairs of students to critique each other's drafts and offer suggestions for improvement. Tell students to refer to Figure 2-2 on page 25 of the Student Edition as a model for their own résumés. You may consider distributing the two sample résumés located on the CD-ROM.

Curriculum Connection: Social Studies

Students may have valuable information about their experiences from their native countries that could be useful when drafting a résumé. Ask students to discuss with English-proficient students any job or educational experiences that could be added to their résumés. Suggest that students should consider highlighting language proficiency in their résumés. Ask English-proficient students to assist students in presenting this information in a useful way.

Job Path Project

Tell students to keep their career choices in mind as they draft their résumés. What special skills can help them compete for a job in their chosen fields? Students may also ask to see the résumés of people in this field so that they can understand what skills are important for them to emphasize.

Writing a Cover Letter

Student Edition, pages 28–31

LEARNING OBJECTIVE

▶ Students will learn how to write a cover letter.

Lesson Resources

On the *CD-ROM*

- Topic at-a-Glance: Reading Classified Ads from a Newspaper

- Topics at-a-Glance: Model Cover Letters 1 and 2

INTO

Using Prior Knowledge

A cover letter introduces a potential employee. Ask students to think about Melody's résumé on page 25 of the Student Edition. Why might a cover letter be useful? Then, ask students to preview the lesson headings and captions and predict what they will learn about writing a cover letter.

THROUGH

Developing the Lesson

This lesson discusses the purpose of cover letters. Students learn how to plan a cover letter, prepare a first draft, and then edit and proofread it. Students also learn that a cover letter is their opportunity to communicate important information about themselves and their skills that are not included on their résumés.

Discussing Visuals Discuss Figure 2-4, *Writing in the Real World: Cover Letter*, on page 30 of the Student Edition. Point out that the writer wrote the letter with a particular job in mind. What kinds of information has Eljay Searles included in his cover letter? Why might an employer find this information useful? How might Eljay rewrite his letter for a different job?

BEYOND

Closing the Lesson

Ask students to use the ad and the chart they completed for the *Apply What You Learn* activity and tell them to write a cover letter. What kinds of information do they want their cover letter to communicate? Why might this information be important to this position?

ESL/LEP Tip

Classified ads may include abbreviations and terms that are new to students learning English. Encourage students to work with English-proficient students to decipher the abbreviations that appear in the classified ads on page 41 of the Student Edition. Tell them to add the abbreviations to their Career Word list.

Job Path Project

Ask students to write a cover letter for one of the job leads that they recorded in their job log. Ask students to plan the kinds of things they want to communicate without repeating the information in their résumés. Tell students to pay attention to the way the ads were worded and to edit and proofread their cover letters. You may suggest that students exchange papers with classmates to critique how clearly their letters are written.

TIP

Because the job search is an active process, tell students that their résumés and cover letters should sound active as well. The use of action verbs helps portray an applicant as positive and enthusiastic.

Lesson Resources

On the *CD-ROM*

- Grammar Workshop Practice: Using Action Verbs in Cover Letters and Résumés
- Grammar Workshop Test: Using Action Verbs in Cover Letters and Résumés
- Handbook Practice: Action, Linking, and Compound Verbs

In the *Handbook*

- Verbs and Verb Forms: 351

Additional Resources From Globe Fearon:

- *Globe Exercise Books* *Parts of Speech*: 8–9

- *Writer's Toolkit* Handbook: Grammar Handbook: Verbs

USING ACTION VERBS IN COVER LETTERS AND RÉSUMÉS

Grammar Workshop at-a-Glance

This Grammar Workshop encourages students to use action verbs in their business writing as a strong way to show their writing skills. Students also learn how to use these verbs in the past tense, in the present tense, and in the future tense.

Error Alert: Solving the Problem

- Write this sentence on the chalkboard: *Manuel did his training.*

- Ask students, *How can you rewrite this sentence using an action verb?* (Manuel completed his training.)

- Write this sentence on the chalkboard: *I came up with a weekend work schedule.*

- Ask students, *How would you rewrite this sentence using an action verb?* (I created a weekend work schedule.)

- Write this sentence on the chalkboard: *I will make the plans for the office holiday party.*

- Ask students, *How would you rewrite this sentence using an action verb?* (I will organize the office holiday party.)

- Write this sentence on the chalkboard: *I always add my input when I am part of a meeting.*

- Ask students, *How would you rewrite this sentence using an action verb?* (I always contribute when I am part of a meeting.)

✎ Write the following sentences on the chalkboard. Ask students to choose an action verb for each sentence. Then, ask students to rewrite each sentence in the past, present, and future tenses.

1. I looked over the new data. (analyzed, am analyzing, will analyze)

2. I told the vendor when to deliver the materials. (instructed, am instructing, will instruct)

3. I worked with the new employees. (trained, am training, will train)

4. I helped start the new company policy. (initiated, am initiating, will initiate)

5. I bettered the working conditions. (improved, am improving, will improve)

Preparing for the Job Interview

Student Edition, pages 33–35

LEARNING OBJECTIVES

▶ Students will learn how to prepare for a successful job interview.

▶ Students will learn to present themselves as polite, professional, and reliable.

Lesson Resources

On the *CD-ROM*

• Topic at-a-Glance: Ten Commonly Asked Interview Questions

• Topic at-a-Glance: Interviewing Techniques Checklist

INTO

Using Prior Knowledge

Ask students who have had job interviews to discuss their experiences. Did they feel prepared? What surprised them? What do they wish they had known? How would they change their interview styles? Ask students to preview the lesson headings and captions and predict what they will learn about getting ready for a job interview.

THROUGH

Developing the Lesson

Students learn that there are two types of job interviews—screening and selection. They learn how to prepare for a successful interview, from gathering an interview packet to learning more about the company to rehearsing answers to possible interview questions. Review the list of interview questions on page 34 of the Student Edition. Then, review the tips for giving good responses. What makes a good response? What are good questions for the interviewee to ask the interviewer?

BEYOND

Closing the Lesson

After students complete the *Apply What You Learn* activity by role-playing their interviews for the class, ask them what they learned about interviewing. Tell students watching the role-play that they should take notes so that they can give each other tips. What kinds of tips can they offer their classmates? What did they do well? What could they improve? How was their body language? How were the interviewer's questions? You may wish to distribute the Interviewing Techniques Checklist and Ten Commonly Asked Interview Questions from the CD-ROM.

ESL/LEP Tip

Ask students to practice responding to the interview questions on page 34 of the Student Edition. Are there any questions that are unclear? Are there any words or phrases in the interview process that are unfamiliar or confusing? Ask English-proficient students to help students to understand and respond to the interview questions. Ask English language learners to think back to any special educational or employment skills they included on their résumés in Lesson 2-2. Ask English-proficient students to help students customize their responses to include this special information.

Evaluating Your Interview Performance

Student Edition, pages 36–38

INTO

Using Prior Knowledge

Ask students how they learn from their experiences. Do they review incorrect test questions to see where they made errors? How do they try to avoid those kinds of errors the next time? Ask students to preview the lesson headings and captions and predict what they will learn about evaluating their interview performance.

THROUGH

Developing the Lesson

This lesson includes a checklist that allows interviewees to evaluate their performances before, during, and after interviews. Encourage students to use the guidelines on page 36 to evaluate their interviews. They also learn that the interview is a valuable experience from which students can learn valuable information about themselves and the interview process. Once students learn how to evaluate their experiences, they learn how to draft follow-up letters.

Discussing Visuals Review Figure 2-6, *Writing in the Real World: Follow-up Letter*, on page 37 of the Student Edition. Discuss the callouts. Why is it important to write a follow-up letter? What should be emphasized in a follow-up letter? What does a follow-up letter tell a prospective employer about the interviewee?

BEYOND

Closing the Lesson

Ask students to write a summary of the key points made by the interviewer they contacted for the *Apply What You Learn* activity. Ask students to share their summaries with the class. Which tips were cited most frequently? Why might following these tips help to impress a potential employer?

Extending the Lesson

Ask students to brainstorm a list of ideas of what they would include in a follow-up letter. What information should be included? What skills and talents should they remind the interviewer that they have?

Job Path Project

Ask students to customize the follow-up letter for an interview they may have gone on or plan to go on. Encourage students to write in a friendly tone, to use action verbs, and to remind the interviewer of the skills and talents they will bring to the job.

Student Edition, pages 42–43

BEING COMPETENT IN THE WORKPLACE
English in Context

TEACHING THE CHAPTER OPENER

Roger works in the copy department of a printing plant. Ms. Bendix, his employer, told him that he is costing the company money because he spends too much time on some projects and not enough on others. Now, he is trying to decide whether he should keep his job or become an entrepreneur and begin his own printing business.

• Being successful at work requires some skills that are not often taught in school. This chapter can help teach these skills, which include teamwork and making decisions. Ask students to look at the lesson titles in this chapter. Talk about which skills students think they have. Then, ask them how these skills might be used differently at work and at school.

PORTFOLIO SETUP: WRITING A BUSINESS PLAN

• On page 61 of the Student Edition, students are asked to write a business plan. Brainstorm possible businesses students might start. Direct students to the list of steps detailed in the Portfolio Project on page 61 of the Student Edition. Ask students to write their answers to each step and show you the list for a critique before they write the final draft of their plans.

CD-ROM TEAMWORK/COOPERATIVE ACTIVITY

• This activity helps students practice conflict resolution. Groups begin by brainstorming conflicts. Then, they choose three of them, describe the attempted resolution, and suggest other ways to resolve the problem. Ask each group to share its conflicts and resolutions with the class.

LESSON PLANNING CHART			
CHAPTER 3	**STUDENT EDITION PAGES**	**TEACHER'S RESOURCE MANUAL PAGES**	**CD-ROM**
Writing/Reading Activities	48, 49, 55, 60–62	16, 18, 19, 21	✓
Speaking/Listening Activities	46, 52, 61	16, 18, 20, 22	✓
Career Activities	44, 46, 52, 56, 58–62	16	✓
Critical Thinking Activities	44, 46–48, 50, 52, 53, 55, 56, 58, 62	16–18, 20, 21	✓
Vocabulary Activities	43, 60		✓
ESL/LEP Tips		20	
Teamwork/Cooperative Activities	46, 52, 61	16, 20, 22	✓
Curriculum Connections		17, 20, 22	
Technology Activities	59, 62	23	

LEARNING OBJECTIVE

▶ Students will learn how to become a valuable member of a team.

Teamwork

Student Edition, pages 44–46

INTO

Using Prior Knowledge

Ask students to talk about teams that they have been a part of. These may range from a student group completing a school project to being a member of the soccer team. What made the teams a success? What problems developed? Ask students to think about how participating in a team at work might be different from being a member of a team at school. Then, ask students to preview the lesson headings and captions and predict what they will learn about teamwork.

THROUGH

Developing the Lesson

This lesson includes a discussion of what teamwork is and the importance of teamwork in the workplace. Students learn about company culture, the benefits of teamwork, essential teamwork skills, the importance of cooperating with others, and how to make teamwork successful.

Discussing Visuals Review with your students Figure 3-1 on page 45 of the Student Edition. Discuss the seven essential teamwork skills. Which of these skills do they do well? Which of them do they need to improve? Review Figure 3-2 on page 46 of the Student Edition. Which personality type do they identify with most closely? How do their personality types affect how they work with others? Ask students how they might handle the following scenarios:

• Locating a lost shipment in a warehouse

• Creating a manual about company procedures

• Deciding on a way to handle a customer complaint

BEYOND

Closing the Lesson

After students complete the *Apply What You Learn* activity, ask the members of each group to evaluate how they worked with one another to complete the assignment. How did each member of the team practice the essential teamwork skills cited in Figure 3-1? What kinds of personality types do team members have? How did the different types help the team?

Curriculum Connection: Science

Ask students to talk about the first time man walked on the moon. Was this the achievement of one person or did a team contribute? Ask students to explain their answers. Then, ask students to think of other examples of achievements that required teamwork.

LESSON 3-2

LEARNING OBJECTIVE

▶ Students will learn how to make effective decisions.

Making Decisions
Student Edition, pages 47–48

INTO

Using Prior Knowledge

Ask students about important decisions they recently made. How did they make them? Explain that decision-making strategies can vary from person to person. Tell students that one person may agonize over the smallest details, while someone else may make a snap decision. Ask students to preview the lesson headings and captions and predict what they will learn about making decisions.

THROUGH

Developing the Lesson

Students learn that there are two different types of decision makers: Information-driven Decision Makers and Action-driven Decision Makers. Ask students to read the definitions of each of these on page 47 of the Student Edition. Which type are they? Then, students learn a step-by-step process that will help them make effective decisions. The steps of the process are having a clear goal, exploring alternatives, narrowing choices, considering the consequences of each possibility, and deciding on a plan of action. Model the decision-making process for the class by discussing a hypothetical decision, such as choosing a research project topic for school.

BEYOND

Closing the Lesson

Ask students to exchange their pictures and explanations from the *Apply What You Learn* activity. Then, ask students to read a colleague's explanation of how he or she would use the five steps to make a decision about buying an item. Based on the explanation, would they have made the same decision? Why or why not?

Extending the Lesson

Tell students that decision making is an important skill that they will use repeatedly at school and on the job. Ask students to identify a decision involving school or work. Then, ask them to use the five-step process outlined on pages 47 and 48 of the Student Edition. Ask volunteers to state the decisions they made and how they arrived at them. Were they easy decisions to make? Did they use all the steps in the decision-making process?

Grammar Workshop

WRITING COMPOUND SENTENCES

Grammar Workshop at-a-Glance

This Grammar Workshop explains that a compound sentence has two or more independent clauses. It explains how to combine clauses using a comma and a conjunction or using a semicolon.

Error Alert: Solving the Problem

- Write this sentence on the chalkboard: *We buy our supplies at the local office supply store we also shop on the Internet.*

- Ask students, *How many complete thoughts are there in this sentence?* (two) *What are they?* (We buy our supplies at the local office supply store. We also shop on the Internet.)

- Ask students, *What is one way to separate these two complete thoughts?* (using a comma and a conjunction: We buy our supplies at the local supply store, and we also shop on the Internet.)

- Ask students, *What is another way to separate these two complete thoughts?* (using a semicolon: We buy our supplies at the local office supply store; we also shop on the Internet.)

- Write this sentence on the chalkboard: *She always has good advice listen to her recommendations.*

- Ask students, *What is one way to separate these two complete thoughts?* (She always has good advice, so listen to her recommendations.)

- Ask students, *What is another way to separate these two complete thoughts?* (She always has good advice; listen to her recommendations.)

Write these sentences on the chalkboard. Ask students to rewrite each sentence first by using a comma and a conjunction and then by using a semicolon.

1. The budget planning was complete it was time to submit our report.

2. The restaurant manager took an inventory he placed next month's food order.

3. The hygienist's assistant confirmed each patient's appointment one patient was late anyway.

4. The Human Resources department organized the company picnic a lot of people attended.

5. Ms. Clark's new assistant reorganized the files it is much easier to find things now.

TIP

Tell students that they can find each independent clause by identifying each complete thought.

Lesson Resources

On the CD-ROM

- Grammar Workshop Practice: Writing Compound Sentences
- Grammar Workshop Test: Writing Compound Sentences
- Handbook Practice: Simple, Compound, and Complex Sentences

In the Handbook

- Sentences: 346

Additional Resources From Globe Fearon:

- *Globe Exercise Books* *Sentences:* 14–15
- *Success in Writing* *Grammar Skills for Writers:* 11

Resolving Conflicts on the Job

Student Edition, pages 50–52

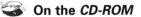
INTO

Using Prior Knowledge

Everyone has dealt with conflicts, but some people have more success resolving them than others. Ask students to share their past experiences with conflict resolution. Were they able to resolve the conflict? How? What methods or rules do they follow when they are trying to resolve problems with others? Encourage students to share their tips for dealing with conflicts. Then, ask students to preview the lesson headings and captions and predict what they will learn about resolving conflicts on the job.

THROUGH

Developing the Lesson

Students learn why conflicts occur as well as strategies for resolving them. They learn that conflicts can occur with customers, with coworkers, and with supervisors; and they also learn what to do when a conflict arises.

Discussing Visuals Discuss the figures on page 51 and page 52 of the Student Edition. Tell students to analyze the body language of the people in each figure. What do these illustration say about resolving conflicts?

BEYOND

Closing the Lesson

Ask each group to role-play the conflict they chose for the *Apply What You Learn* activity for the entire class. Once a group finishes role-playing its conflict, ask the members of the group what resolution they suggested. Then, ask the class to suggest how the conflict can be resolved. What would they have done differently to resolve the conflict? How is one solution more effective than the other?

ESL/LEP Tip

Different cultures deal with conflict in very different ways. Ask students to discuss how conflicts are resolved in their native countries. How is conflict resolution in their countries similar to the approach outlined in this lesson? How is it different? Ask students to explain how one of the situations that was role-played in *Closing the Lesson* may have been resolved in their countries.

Curriculum Connection: Social Studies

Ask students to look through a newspaper or magazine and identify a news story that revolves around a conflict. Ask students to suggest a resolution to the conflict.

Organizing Your Work

Student Edition, pages 53–55

LEARNING OBJECTIVE

▶ Students will learn how to organize their work efficiently.

Lesson Resources

On the *CD-ROM*

• Topic at-a-Glance: Organizing Your Work

• Application: Organizing Your Work

INTO

Using Prior Knowledge

Almost everyone has problems with organization. Ask students to talk about their problems with organization. What strategies do they use to organize their work? Then, ask students to preview the lesson headings and captions and predict what they will learn about organizing their work.

THROUGH

Developing the Lesson

This lesson focuses on how students can organize their work. The lesson addresses the need to be organized and lists some benefits of being organized, such as having control of your work, knowing you will be able to finish your work, having control over your job performance, and feeling confident. Students learn that businesses value an organized employee. Students also learn five steps that help them to manage their time.

Discussing Visuals Review Figure 3-3, *Writing in the Real World: Daily Planner*, on page 54 of the Student Edition. Discuss the callouts with students. How is a daily planner an effective organizational tool? What are some other ways to prioritize tasks?

BEYOND

Closing the Lesson

Ask students to review the lists they compiled for the *Apply What You Learn* activity. How well did they prioritize their tasks? Did they follow the five steps outlined on page 55 of the Student Edition? Then, discuss how scheduling a week's worth of tasks can help keep priorities in order. Ask students to organize their schoolwork for one week. At the end of the week, ask students how useful their lists were. Did their lists help them to remember important tasks that needed to be completed? What might they do differently with the lists to make it even more useful?

Extending the Lesson

Ask students to recall Roger's situation on page 42 of the Student Edition. Now that students have learned the importance of organizing their work, managing their time, and prioritizing their tasks, ask them to respond to Roger's situation. What kind of advice can they give him so that he can avoid spending too much time on some jobs and not enough on others? What can Roger do to manage his workload?

Being an Entrepreneur
Student Edition, pages 56–58

INTO

Using Prior Knowledge

Ask students to describe any businesses they have started on their own, such as baby-sitting or mowing lawns. What skills do they think are the most important for successful entrepreneurs? Ask students to preview the lesson headings and captions and predict what they will learn about being entrepreneurs.

THROUGH

Developing the Lesson

This lesson describes the traits that entrepreneurs share. Students learn about the advantages and disadvantages of entrepreneurship. They also learn the steps involved in becoming an entrepreneur, as well as in buying a business and running a franchise.

Discussing Visuals Review Figure 3-4 on page 56 of the Student Edition. Ask students to list each of the categories and rate themselves from 1 to 5. Tell students that 1 represents the information on the left side of the OR and 5 represents the information on the right side of the OR. Do they need a big push or are they self-starters who take the initiative? Ask students to discuss how their combinations of qualities may or may not be suitable for entrepreneurship.

BEYOND

Closing the Lesson

After students have completed the charts for the *Apply What You Learn* activity, ask them to exchange them with a classmate and critique their classmates's charts. Have all the advantages and disadvantages been considered? Is their classmate's marketing plan an effective one? Ask them to explain their answers.

Curriculum Connections: Math

Ask students to research the math skills they would need to run their own businesses. Students should consider computing payrolls, ordering supplies, maintaining budgets, and other accounting-related activities. Ask students to report what they learn.

Web Activity

Ask students to think back to the business they chose for the *Apply What You Learn* activity on page 58 of the Student Edition. Ask students to search the Internet for possible sites that could help promote their businesses. For example, if students are starting a pet-grooming business, they could link to a site that sells pet supplies. How else can the Internet help entrepreneurs promote their businesses?

TECH CONNECTIONS

The Fax Machine
(Student Edition, page 17)

Bring to class examples of faxes that have been sent. Explain that hand-written notes may not be legible, and colors, such as red, may turn black when faxed. Point out the features of the cover page. Explain that the cover sheet allows the recipient to determine whether or not all the pages were received. If students have access to fax machines, ask students to practice sending and receiving faxes. Which images faxed successfully? Which did not?

Internet Job Search
(Student Edition, page 39)

Explain to students that there are numerous Web sites that specialize in helping people find jobs. Once students complete the Application on page 39 of the Student Edition, ask them which Web site they found most useful and which one they found least useful. Why? What kind of information was the least useful site lacking? Encourage students to use the helpful sites as additional resources when conducting their job searches.

Develop a Spreadsheet
(Student Edition, page 59)

Ask students when they might need to use a spreadsheet. For example, students could use a spreadsheet for their personal finances or to run a department of a small business. You might consider asking students to work in groups to finish the Application activity. They can work together to decide on a type of business, its expenses, and projected profits, and place the information in the spreadsheet program. How does the spread-sheet help to organize the information?

Additional Resource
From Globe Fearon:

Survival Guide for Computer Literacy: 79, 100

THE PATH TO WRITING SUCCESS

Student Edition, page 63

CAREER FILE PROJECT SUPPORT

On page 106 of the Student Edition, students will read about chefs and medical records technicians. While the job of a chef may be familiar to students, they may not have thought about what it means to be a medical records technician. Explain that health records are a critical part of any doctor's office or hospital. Ask students to think about the kinds of skills a person might need to perform in this job. Tell students who are interested in either of these careers to arrange a job-shadowing opportunity. Students can record their experience using the job-shadowing application on the CD-ROM.

Action Profile

Ask students to choose one of the two careers profiled in this unit and answer the following questions:

1. What experience, education, and training do employers expect of those they hire?
2. Are there any local or state requirements for working in this field?
3. What interests and traits do you have that would make this a good job for you?
4. Does the job have any requirements you might have difficulty meeting?
5. What related fields might interest you?

This unit is essential reading for students who want to improve their writing skills. The unit covers the basic steps in the writing process: prewriting, drafting, editing, proofreading, and publishing. Students will learn how to integrate the steps of the writing process with the writing they will be doing when they join the workforce.

What's in the Unit

In Unit 2, students are introduced to the steps of the writing process: prewriting, drafting, editing, proofreading, and publishing. They learn how to identify their audience, formulate a topic, and collect and organize information. This unit teaches the different stages of the writing process that students will need to know to be able to handle any writing assignment.

Previewing the Unit

Many high school students find writing to be a challenge. Often, they stare at the blank page and are uncertain of how to begin. Tell students that this unit will give them the tools they need to write effectively from planning to publication. Ask students to preview the unit by looking at the titles, headings, subheadings, figures, photos, illustrations, captions, and key words. Then, ask them to predict what they will learn in this unit. Why is writing an important skill at school, in life, and on the job?

Developing the Unit

Ask students to suppose that they have to write an important business report for their employer. Ask them how they would begin. What is the first thing they would need to do? What steps would they follow? After the class brainstorms ideas, ask students to write the steps. Then, have students identify the steps of the writing process listed in the book, and ask them to compare what they wrote to the notes they compiled in their KWL chart while previewing the unit.

ACTIVITY	MINUTES
Preview lesson headings, captions, and boldfaced words; five-minute free-write on how students plan and execute major writing assignments	10
Read and discuss Lessons 4-1 and 4-2	20
Small groups meet to discuss *Apply What You Learn*, Lesson 4-1	10
Writing: Work on Job Path Project; report on area of interest	20
Discuss Workplace Workshop: Phrases and Clauses	15
Small groups meet to discuss *Apply What You Learn*, Lesson 4-2	10
Concluding reflections, assignments, answer questions	5

IN-DEPTH DISCOVERY
Resources for students to explore include

- *The Plain English Approach to Business Writing* by Edward P. Bailey, Jr. and Larry Bailey. New York: Oxford University Press, 1997. This book shows readers how to improve the quality and clarity of their business writing.

- *Vest-Pocket Guide to Business Writing: The Instant-Answer Source for Today's Business Writer* by Deborah Dumaine. New York: Prentice Hall, 1997. This reference provides hundreds of writing tips, over 30 model documents, and answers to business writing questions.

- *Write to the Point! Letters, Memos, and Reports That Get Results* by Rosemary T. Fruehling and N. B. Oldham. New York: McGraw-Hill, 1997. This book offers advice on writing letters, reports, and memos for nonprofessional writers.

Within the Family
Writing is a part of virtually every job. Emphasize this for students by asking them to interview adult workers in their family or community about the types of writing they are required to do on the job. Ask students to share their findings with the rest of the class. List the various work-related writing assignments on the chalkboard.

Job Path Project
Students should now have identified the career areas that most interest them. Ask students to write a report about the career or job in which they are most interested. Students can keep their completed reports as part of their portfolio.

Discussing the Quote
Ask students to read the quote by Gloria Estefan on page 63 of the Student Edition. How does this quote relate to the writing process?

Closing the Unit
When students complete this unit, they should be able to use the writing process in a variety of situations both at school and on the job. To reinforce their knowledge of this process, ask students to write a one-page summary of the writing steps. Then, ask them to paste it inside their notebooks so that they can use the summary as a reference any time they are assigned writing projects. As students complete each chapter in this unit, you can use the chapter assessments located on the CD-ROM to check their progress.

Student Edition, pages 64–65

BEGINNING THE WRITING PROCESS
English in Context

TEACHING THE CHAPTER OPENER

Kai has been accepted into a management training program. However, she is hesitant to write the paper about her goals that is required of all trainees. She knows what her goals are, but she is still apprehensive about the writing process. This chapter offers a way to begin the writing process, because this can be the most difficult step for students.

• Ask your students to offer Kai advice on how can she begin to write the paper about herself and her goals.

PORTFOLIO SETUP: WRITING ABOUT GOALS

• On page 83 of the Student Edition, students are asked to write about their goals. Students choose one career goal from the list they assembled in Unit 1 and prepare a piece of writing that explains how they could achieve this goal. On the chalkboard, write the steps of the writing process that are discussed in this chapter: determine your audience, narrow your topic, and gather and organize your ideas. (See the CD-ROM for various graphic organizers.) Ask students to follow the steps of the writing process to prepare their reports.

CD-ROM TEAMWORK/COOPERATIVE ACTIVITY

• This activity offers practice working with a research group. Each member of the group chooses one of the following tasks: select a topic and audience, collect information, organize the information, and make an oral presentation. Then, the group combines its findings and presents them to its audience.

LESSON PLANNING CHART

CHAPTER 4	STUDENT EDITION PAGES	TEACHER'S RESOURCE MANUAL PAGES	CD-ROM
Writing/Reading Activities	69, 70, 72, 74, 75, 80–83	26–29, 31, 32, 34	✓
Speaking/Listening Activities	67, 69, 74	26, 28, 30	✓
Career Activities	83	31	✓
Critical Thinking Activities	66, 71, 73, 76, 79, 82, 83	26, 27, 30, 31, 33	✓
Vocabulary Activities	65, 82	27	✓
ESL/LEP Tips		27, 28, 33	
Teamwork/Cooperative Activities	69, 74	26	✓
Curriculum Connections		30	
Technology Activities	81	30, 43	✓

Understanding the Writing Process

Student Edition, pages 66–67

LEARNING OBJECTIVE

❱ Students will understand the steps of the writing process.

Lesson Resource

📖 **In the *Handbook***

• The Writing Process: 337

INTO

Using Prior Knowledge

Ask students what they usually do when they are faced with a major writing assignment. What do they do first? What do they do next? Ask students to preview the lesson headings and captions and predict what they will learn about the writing process.

THROUGH

Developing the Lesson

This lesson offers an overview of the steps of the writing process: prewriting, drafting, editing, proofreading, and publishing. Students learn that these writing steps are not linear because writers may go back and forth between different steps until they are satisfied with their work. Ask students how this differs from what they usually do when they are given a writing assignment.

Discussing Visuals Refer to Figures 4-1 and 4-2 on pages 66 and 67 to clarify the steps of the writing process. Point out that good writers think about these steps every time they write. List examples of the different kinds of writing that students might do in school, such as an English report or a biology lab report, or in business, such as an e-mail, a sales report, or a response to a complaint. Discuss how the writing process applies to each one.

BEYOND

Closing the Lesson

Students can continue to work individually on the *Apply What You Learn* activity. Ask each student to make a chart or Venn diagram (see the CD-ROM for a reproducible graphic organizer) that shows which process the student investigated. What are the advantages to this process? What are the disadvantages to this process?

ESL/LEP Tip

Students learning English need to understand the terms that describe the writing process. Ask these students to work with an English-proficient student to write definitions for prewriting, drafting, editing, proofreading, and publishing. Have students add these definitions to their personal dictionaries.

Additional Resources From Globe Fearon:

• *Success in Writing*
Writing to Describe: 75
Writing to Explain: 75
Writing to Persuade: 75
Grammar Skills for Writers: 118

• *Writer's Toolkit*
Handbook: Writing Handbook: The Writing Process

Deciding the Purpose and Audience

Student Edition, pages 68–69

INTO

Using Prior Knowledge

To produce a focused piece of writing, every writer must begin with a purpose and an audience in mind. The things you write have a purpose, and it is important to consider who you are writing to. Ask students to preview the lesson headings and captions and predict what they will learn about deciding the purpose and audience.

THROUGH

Developing the Lesson

In this lesson, students will learn the four main reasons for writing: to inform, to explain, to describe, and to persuade. Students will also learn how their audience affects how they plan and write.

Discussing Visuals Discuss the information in Figure 4-4 on page 69 of the Student Edition. Ask students how they would approach a writing task for a particular audience. To reinforce this discussion, write the following topics on the chalkboard: a letter from a student to a teacher asking for a recommendation, a recommendation for a friend seeking a job, and an explanation of a procedure on the job. Ask students to consider the audience and purpose for each type of writing. How would they approach each of these writing tasks?

BEYOND

Closing the Lesson

Ask students to complete the *Apply What You Learn* activity, making a grid that lists the audience, the purpose, and the reason for choosing that purpose. Ask students to write a letter about a toy that might be sent to one of the audiences identified on the grid. Have students share their letters with their class.

ESL/LEP Tip

Make sure students learning English understand why the tone of a person's writing varies based on the audience. Work with them on a writing assignment in which they write a paragraph inviting the general public to the Green Avenue Fair. The paragraph should be written as if the students are organizing the fair. The paragraph should include pertinent information, such as location, time, and the kinds of activities in which the general public can expect to participate.

TIP

Tell students that there is an effective way to identify phrases. Explain that phrases do not contain a subject and a predicate and cannot stand alone. If a group of words has both a subject and predicate, it is a clause, not a phrase.

Lesson Resources

On the *CD-ROM*

- Grammar Workshop Practice: Using Clauses and Phrases
- Grammar Workshop Test: Using Clauses and Phrases
- Handbook Practice: Independent and Dependent Clauses

In the *Handbook*

- Clauses: 347
- Phrases: 347

Additional Resources From Globe Fearon:

- *Globe Exercise Books*
  Sentences: 28–35

- *Writer's Toolkit*
  Handbook: Grammar
  Handbook: Clauses and Phrases and Sentence Structure

USING CLAUSES AND PHRASES

Grammar Workshop at-a-Glance

This Grammar Workshop focuses on phrases and clauses. Phrases are groups of words that do not contain a subject and a predicate and cannot stand alone. Independent clauses are groups of words that contain a subject and a predicate, express a complete thought, and can stand alone. Dependent clauses contain a subject and a verb, do not express a complete thought, and cannot stand alone.

Error Alert: Solving the Problem

- Write this phrase on the chalkboard: *The discussion*

- Ask students, *Is this correct?* (no) *How can we make this phrase a complete thought?* (The discussion lasted all night.)

- Write this phrase on the chalkboard: *Ran home*

- Ask students, *Is this correct?* (no) *How can we make this phrase a complete thought?* (The dog ran home.)

- Write this phrase on the chalkboard: *Until we arrive*

- Ask students, *Is this correct?* (no) *How can we correct this?* (Until we arrive, they cannot get started.)

- Write this phrase on the chalkboard: *Because she stayed late*

- Ask students, *Is this correct?* (no) *How can we correct this?* (Because she stayed late, the team made its deadline.)

✎ Write the following phrases and dependent clauses on the chalkboard. Then, ask students to make them into complete sentences.

1. Along the narrow corridor

2. Because he was there

3. While compiling the report

4. Before going to lunch

5. After everything that happened

Choosing and Narrowing a Topic

Student Edition, pages 71–72

LEARNING OBJECTIVE

❱ Students will learn how to choose and narrow a topic before writing.

Lesson Resources

 On the CD-ROM

• Topic at-a-Glance: Choosing and Narrowing a Topic

• Application: Choosing and Narrowing a Topic

Additional Resources From Globe Fearon:

• *Success in Writing*
  Writing to Describe: 19–21, 40
  Writing to Explain: 20–22
  Writing to Persuade: 20–22

• *Writer's Toolkit*
  Choosing a Topic: Issues Wheel, Research Paper Topic Bin; Narrowing a Topic: Topic Web, Cluster Diagram

INTO

Using Prior Knowledge

When students choose and narrow a topic, they are able to avoid some common problems. Ask students if they have ever ended up with uninteresting topics; chose broad topics that were not focused, and their papers wandered; or their topics were too narrow, and there was not enough research information to write a paper. How did they handle this? Ask students to preview the lesson headings and captions and predict what they will learn about choosing and narrowing a topic.

THROUGH

Developing the Lesson

In this lesson, students will learn ways to sharpen their writing focus by choosing and narrowing a topic.

Discussing Visuals Review Figure 4-5 on page 72 of the Student Edition to show students how a writing topic was limited. Then, ask students to work in pairs to discuss how they might approach the following topics: providing a company history, announcing a new product, or reporting annual sales figures. Are these topics too narrow? too broad? a reasonable size? Ask students to make suggestions for broadening narrow topics and narrowing broad topics. Have students explain why some topics seem to be manageable.

BEYOND

Closing the Lesson

Ask students to record the process they went through to narrow each broad topic they chose in the *Apply What You Learn* activity into a manageable topic. How did they approach the task of narrowing each topic? What did they take into consideration about each broader topic? Why?

Curriculum Connection: Science

Ask students to think about the kinds of science topics that they would need to narrow. How would you approach the task of narrowing a topic like the moon? chemistry?

Web Activity

Ask students to think about the approach they suggested for narrowing a topic such as "the moon." If students have access to the Internet, ask them to do a topic search on the moon. Why is it important to narrow a topic prior to searching it on the Web?

Collecting Information
Student Edition, pages 73–74

INTO
Using Prior Knowledge
Ask students to make a quick list of sources they use when they have to write a report. Have students share their lists with the rest of the class. Discuss the advantages and disadvantages of each resource. Then, ask students to preview the lesson headings and captions and predict what they will learn about collecting information.

THROUGH
Developing the Lesson
In this lesson, students learn that the most important sources of information are books and magazines, the Internet, and experienced people. Students also learn how to assess the reliability of sources. You can use this lesson to provide students with practical research skills.

Discussing Visuals Discuss the section entitled Sources of Information on pages 73-74 of the Student Edition. Ask students how the checklist on page 74 can help them evaluate research sources.

BEYOND
Closing the Lesson
Ask students to take the *Apply What You Learn* activity one step further and justify their reasons for choosing particular sources. What makes each of the sources that students chose a helpful research tool?

Job Path Project
Ask students to research the career that they have chosen for their Job Path Project. In their search, students should find at least one book, one magazine article, one Internet source, and one knowledgeable person. Ask students to rate the reliability of the sources by using the checklist on page 74 in the Student Edition. Students' resources will serve as the foundations for their career reports.

Extending the Lesson
Ask students to devise a system for keeping track of the sources they find. Suggest that coding index cards in different colors can be useful. Each color can represent a particular source of information. Yellow index cards can represent Source A, blue index cards can represent Source B, and so on. Students could also use a different array of highlighters to code index cards, computer printouts, or photocopies.

LEARNING OBJECTIVE

▶ Students will learn how to collect information before writing.

Lesson Resources

On the *CD-ROM*

- Topic at-a-Glance: Sources of Information
- Application: Collecting Information

Additional Resources From Globe Fearon:

- *Success in Writing*
  Writing to Explain: 25, 70
  Writing to Persuade: 26

- *Writer's Toolkit*
  Handbook: Writing
  Handbook: Elements of Nonfiction: Using Resources

Grammar Workshop

TIP

Remind students that the *and* in *Leo and Martin* signals a plural subject. However, if the subject were *Leo or Martin*, the *or* signals a singular subject.

Lesson Resources

 **On the *CD-ROM***

- Grammar Workshop Practice: Making Subjects and Verbs Agree
- Grammar Workshop Test: Making Subjects and Verbs Agree
- Handbook Practice: Subject-Verb Agreement

In the *Handbook*

- Subject-Verb Agreement: 347–348

Additional Resources From Globe Fearon:

- *Globe Exercise Books*
  Mechanics and Usage: 4–5
  Parts of Speech: 16–17
  Sentences: 22–23

- *Success in Writing*
  Grammar Skills for Writers: 57–59

- *Writer's Toolkit*
  Handbook: Grammar
  Handbook: Subject-Verb Agreement

MAKING SUBJECTS AND VERBS AGREE

Grammar Workshop at-a-Glance

Lack of agreement between subjects and their verbs is a common error. In this workshop, students learn to look only at the subject and verb when trying to determine subject-verb agreement.

Error Alert: Solving the Problem

Often, students do not know how to find the subject and the verb in a sentence. Use the following technique to help students understand subject-verb agreement.

- Write this sentence on the chalkboard: *Mr. Barr help the customers in his store.*

- Ask students, *Is this sentence correct?* (no) *How can we correct this?* (*help* should be *helps*)

- Write this sentence on the chalkboard: *His colleague, who organized the seminar, work in the marketing department.*

- Ask students, *Is this sentence correct?* (no) *How can we correct this?* (*work* should be *works*)

- Write this sentence on the chalkboard: *Both Greg and Michael gets extra responsibility at the office.*

- Ask students, *Is this sentence correct?* (no) *How can we correct this?* (*gets* should be *get*)

Write the following sentences on the chalkboard. Ask students to underline the subject once and the verb twice. Have them draw an arrow from the subject to the verb. Ask students to say the subject and the verb together and decide whether or not they agree with each other. If they do not agree, ask students to write the correct form of the verb.

1. Bob are my boss. (subject: Bob; verb: is)

2. Mary, one of the managers, do most of the work. (subject: Mary; verb: does)

3. My co-worker, who lives near the others, commute with me. (subject: co-worker; verb: commutes)

4. The computers on the table is not working. (subject: computers; verb: are)

5. The videotapes and the book was not returned to the library. (subject: videotapes, book; verb: were)

Organizing Your Information

Student Edition, pages 76–79

LEARNING OBJECTIVE

▶ Students will learn how to organize information before writing.

Lesson Resources

On the CD-ROM

- Topic at-a-Glance: Organizing Your Information
- Application: Chronological Order
- Application: Spatial Order
- Application: Order of Importance
- Application: Cause-and-Effect Order
- Application: Comparison-and-Contrast Order
- Various graphic organizers

In the Handbook

- Strategies for Organizing Your Writing: 338–339

Additional Resources From Globe Fearon:

- *Globe Exercise Books*
  Paragraphs: 16–21
- *Success in Writing*
  Writing to Describe: 27, 43–44, 63–64, 70
  Writing to Explain: 10, 25, 48, 57
  Writing to Persuade: 27
- *Be a Better Reader*
  Level G: 170–171
- *Writer's Toolkit*
  Organizing Details: Timeline and Venn Diagram

INTO

Using Prior Knowledge

Organizing information is as important for the writing process as it is for day-to-day tasks. Explain to students that it allows them to see the relationships between things that do not seem connected. Ask students to preview the lesson headings and captions and predict what they will learn about organizing their information.

THROUGH

Developing the Lesson

In this lesson, students learn five ways to organize information: chronological order, spatial order, order of importance, cause-and-effect order, and comparison-and-contrast order. The lesson also describes how to use more than one organizational method in a piece of writing.

Discussing Visuals Review Figures 4-6, 4-7, 4-8, 4-9, and 4-10 on pages 76 and 77 of the Student Edition. Ask students which method they would use to organize information for each of the following: recording the steps of making a sandwich (chronological order); illustrating the physical layout of a CD store (spatial order); prioritizing workplace tasks (order of importance); describing what happened when a dissatisfied customer asked for a refund and was accommodated by a sales clerk (cause-and-effect order); discussing the differences between "good" and "bad" service (comparison-and-contrast order). Review Figure 4-11, *Writing in the Real World: Methods of Organizing*, on page 78 of the Student Edition. How can a piece of writing be different if it is organized in different ways?

BEYOND

Closing the Lesson

To give students practice using more than one organizational method, ask students to choose one of the topics from the *Apply What You Learn* activity on page 79 of the Student Edition. Ask students to choose two organizational methods for their topics and to explain why they chose each method. Ask students how they would combine these methods in a paper. Why does such a combination work?

ESL/LEP Tip

Suggest that students copy the diagrams in this lesson into their notebooks, with labels written both in their native language and in English.

Grammar Workshop

TIP

Explain to students that using only short sentences can make writing choppy. Readers may even have a hard time telling which ideas are related to one another. Tell students that combining sentences helps make writing smoother and gives it more variety and interest.

Lesson Resources

On the *CD-ROM*

• Grammar Workshop Practice: Writing Complex Sentences

• Grammar Workshop Test: Writing Complex Sentences

• Handbook Practice: Simple, Compound, and Complex Sentences

In the *Handbook*

• Complex Sentences: 346

Additional Resources From Globe Fearon:

• *Globe Exercise Books* *Sentences*: 16–17

• *Success in Writing* *Grammar Skills for Writers*: 12

WRITING COMPLEX SENTENCES

Grammar Workshop at-a-Glance

This workshop explains how to write complex sentences that have one independent clause and one or more dependent clauses. Students learn words that can introduce dependent clauses.

Error Alert: Solving the Problem

Many sentence fragments result when students write dependent clauses and think they are sentences. One way to rectify this mistake is to remove the introductory word that signals the clause as dependent.

• Write this clause on the chalkboard: *Although we got the report in when it was due.*

• Ask students, *Does this sentence express a complete thought? What seems unclear about this sentence?* (*Although* refers to something that is not answered by the sentence; it signals an incomplete thought.) *What is the introductory word, or the word that comes at the beginning of this group of words?* (Although)

• Ask students to read the sentence without the introductory word. *Does it have a subject?* (we) *Does it have a verb?* (got) *Does it express a complete thought?* (yes)

Write the following fragments on the chalkboard. Ask students to identify the introductory word. Then, ask students to recite the words without the introductory word, thereby creating a sentence.

1. Because I had to finish my assignment by Friday

2. Before we were set to begin the new procedure

3. When I was ready to open the store

4 Until my boss explained the situation

5. Whenever we left

6. While the management team was on vacation

7. Before we begin the workday

8. Until they are ready to admit their errors

9. Although he was entirely capable of making the revisions himself

10. Since I finished my report

Student Edition, pages 84–85

COMPLETING THE WRITING PROCESS
English in Context

TEACHING THE CHAPTER OPENER

Davenne, who works in a small, family-owned restaurant, has been given an unusual assignment by her employer. He has asked her to write a new menu. Davenne knows if she does a good job, she may be promoted. Point out to students that jobs often require good writing skills. In this chapter, they will learn to put together the steps involved in creating a piece of writing—from first draft to publication.

• What kinds of writing assignments have students completed? Perhaps they had to write a flyer for a business they worked for or a letter to a prospective employer. Discuss the different kinds of writing that students have created in school, on the job, or in their personal lives.

PORTFOLIO SETUP: WRITING A PRODUCT DESCRIPTION

• On page 105 of the Student Edition, students are asked to write a product description. Ask students to choose a product that they use every day, such as a notebook, a computer, or a microwave oven. Then, ask them to prepare a 200-word product description. Tell students to follow the outline of the lessons in this chapter when writing the product description—prewriting, drafting, editing, proofreading, and publishing.

CD-ROM TEAMWORK/COOPERATIVE ACTIVITY

• This activity provides additional practice using the steps of the writing process. The assignment asks groups to describe a special event or program. The tasks are divided so that there are five jobs—prewriters, drafters, editors, proofreaders, and publishers. One or more students could assume a particular role. This activity can also be used as a framework for topics chosen by you or by the individual groups.

LESSON PLANNING CHART

CHAPTER 5	STUDENT EDITION PAGES	TEACHER'S RESOURCE MANUAL PAGES	CD-ROM
Writing/Reading Activities	89, 90, 94, 95, 99, 100, 104–106	35–42	✓
Speaking/Listening Activities	94, 101, 105	35, 36, 38, 42	✓
Career Activities	105, 106	35, 36, 38, 42	✓
Critical Thinking Activities	86, 89, 91, 94, 96, 101, 104, 105	35, 36, 38, 40	✓
Vocabulary Activities	85, 104		✓
ESL/LEP Tips		36, 40, 42	
Teamwork/Cooperative Activities	94, 101	38, 40	✓
Curriculum Connections		40	
Technology Activities	103	43	

Creating a Draft
Student Edition, pages 86–89

LEARNING OBJECTIVE

▶ Students will learn how to create a draft.

Lesson Resources

On the *CD-ROM*
• Topic at-a-Glance: Creating a Draft

In the *Handbook*
• The Writing Process: 337

INTO
Using Prior Knowledge
Drafting is the writer's first chance to get his or her ideas onto paper. Have small groups preview pages 86–89 of the Student Edition. Ask students to preview lesson headings and captions and predict what they will learn about creating a first draft.

THROUGH
Developing the Lesson
In this lesson, students learn how to create a first draft. They learn to focus on main ideas and to include supporting details.

Discussing Visuals Discuss Figure 5-3, *Writing in the Real World: First Draft*, on page 88, to review the kinds of supporting details, such as facts, examples, incidents, sensory details, and reasons. Ask students to practice identifying main ideas and details by locating main ideas and details in the lesson. For example, ask students what the main idea of the lesson is. (*creating a draft*) Then, ask students to find the supporting details that show how to create a draft. What is prewriting? What happens during the drafting stage of the writing process? How do they think a first draft differs from a finished paper?

BEYOND
Closing the Lesson
Review Figure 5-3 on page 88 of the Student Edition with students. Then, ask them to complete the *Apply What You Learn* activity by reading their tips to the class. Students should discuss what they like about each draft and what they think needs revision to improve clarity. Are some drafts more detailed than others? Does this make them more useful?

ESL/LEP Tip
Students may be unfamiliar with the concept of sensory details. Ask students to bring to class photographs from magazines. Have students exchange photographs. Then, ask students to make a grid with the five senses—sight, sound, touch, smell, and taste—listed across the top. Ask students to look at their photograph and record one or two details for each of the five senses.

Job Path Project
Students have gathered information on their careers of choice. Now, they can work at home on a first draft of their report on this career. Suggest they use this book as a reference as they work.

Additional Resources From Globe Fearon:

• *Globe Exercise Books*
 Paragraphs: 14–15
 Spelling and Vocabulary: 38–39

• *Success in Writing*
 Writing to Describe: 8–9, 12, 25–26, 28–31, 40
 Writing to Explain: 16, 28–32
 Writing to Persuade: 29–32

• *Writer's Toolkit*
 Drafting: Descriptive Word Bin

TIP

Tell students that it is probably easiest to look for transitions when they are revising. Explain that they can add transition words where their ideas seem to shift too quickly.

Lesson Resources

On the *CD-ROM*

- Grammar Workshop Practice: Using Transition Words
- Grammar Workshop Test: Using Transition Words

In the *Handbook*

- Transition Words: 341, 345

Additional Resources From Globe Fearon:

- *Success in Writing*
  Writing to Explain: 14–15
  Grammar Skills for Writers: 90

- *Writer's Toolkit*
  Drafting: Transition Word Bin; Revising and Editing: Transition Word Checker

- *Be a Better Reader*
  Level G: 117

USING TRANSITION WORDS

Grammar Workshop at-a-Glance

In this Grammar Workshop, students learn how to use transition words to show the relationships between ideas in terms of time, additional information, contrasts, examples, and results. Transition words can also be used to make a connection between sentences.

Error Alert: Solving the Problem

- Write this sentence on the chalkboard: *I finished the report on time; unfortunately, it's ready to distribute.*

- Ask students, *Is this correct?* (No; it is not unfortunate that the report is ready to distribute.) *How can we correct this?* (*Unfortunately* should be changed to *so* or *therefore*.)

- Write this sentence on the chalkboard: *Suzie loves working with people; however, she accepted a job where she deals with the public.*

- Ask students, *Is this correct?* (no) *How can we correct this?* (*However* should be changed to *so* or *therefore*.)

- Write this sentence on the chalkboard: *She is a trained architect; morever, she spends a lot of her time answering design questions instead of designing buildings.*

- Ask students, *Is this correct?* (no) *How can we correct this?* (*Moreover* should be changed to *however*.)

- Write this sentence on the chalkboard: *The restaurant manager asks his staff to arrive early; the later they arrive, the more time they have to prepare for their customers.*

- Ask students, *Is this correct?* (no) *How can we correct this?* (*Later* should be changed to *earlier*.)

- Write the following sentences on the chalkboard. Ask students to complete the following sentences using a transition word or phrase.

  1. She got the raise _____ (after) she completed her training.

  2. We know our customers; _____ (as a result,) we are willing to do what it takes to make them happy.

  3. First, we will do the research, and _____ (then) we will make our recommendations.

  4. He is a good worker, _____ (but) he has been late three times this week.

Editing the Draft

Student Edition, pages 91–94

LEARNING OBJECTIVE

▶ Students will learn how to edit a first draft.

Lesson Resources

On the *CD-ROM*

- Topic at-a-Glance: Editing the Draft
- Application: Editing the Draft

In the *Handbook*

- Editing Questionnaire: 340

Additional Resources From Globe Fearon:

- *Globe Exercise Books*
  Paragraphs: 24–33

- *Success in Writing*
  Writing to Describe: 33–34
  Writing to Explain: 33–35
  Grammar Skills for Writers: 103–107
  Writing to Persuade: 34–35

- *Writer's Toolkit*
  Revising and Editing: Unity and Coherence Checker, Sentence-Length Checker

INTO

Using Prior Knowledge

In the editing stage, writers take a second look at what they have written to see if they have achieved their purpose. Ask students what steps they take when they edit their writing. As the class brainstorms answers, write their responses on the chalkboard. Then, ask them to preview the headings and captions and predict what they will learn about editing the draft.

THROUGH

Developing the Lesson

Editing involves checking for the intended audience and purpose, the quality of development and organization, unity and coherence, and word choice.

Discussing Visuals Review Figure 5-6, *Writing in the Real World: Revision*, on page 93 of the Student Edition. How does Kendra's revision differ from her first draft? Does her revision address the questions in Figure 5-5 on page 92 of the Student Edition?

BEYOND

Closing the Lesson

Working in pairs or in small groups, students should continue working on the *Apply What You Learn* activity by making a chart and recording how audience and purpose, quality of development and organization, unity and coherence, and word choice were addressed in Kendra's second draft on page 93 of the Student Edition. What did Kendra do in her second draft that showed she took audience and purpose into consideration? How did Kendra address word choice in her revision?

Extending the Lesson

You can reinforce the importance of revising by creating a poster based on Figure 5-5 on page 92 of the Student Edition. How can asking the questions in Figure 5-5 when revising a draft make subsequent drafts more effective? Use a writing sample to show how students would make each revision. Hang the poster on a wall in the classroom.

Job Path Project

Ask students to edit their Career reports. Tell them to use the revision questions for purpose and audience, quality of development and organization, unity and coherence, and word choice shown in Figure 5-5 on page 92 of the Student Edition. Ask students to give one example of how they addressed each of the categories in Figure 5-5.

Student Edition, page 95

AVOIDING DANGLING MODIFIERS

Grammar Workshop at-a-Glance

This Grammar Workshop deals with dangling modifiers, which are phrases that are unconnected to the rest of the sentence. The Grammar Workshop helps students to identify dangling modifiers and then rewrite the sentence to accurately express its meaning.

Error Alert: Solving the Problem

- Write this sentence on the chalkboard: *After revising the work order, a power outage knocked out the phones.*

- Ask students, *Who revised the work order? Did the power outage revise the order?* (no) *Because that does not make sense, which group of words is the dangling modifier?* (After revising the work order)

- *What is the sentence really trying to tell us? Who or what revised the order?* (*I,* or the speaker of the sentence, revised the order; it could also be someone from the previous sentence.)

- *Because we know that the speaker is the one who revised the order, how can we rewrite the sentence so that the meaning is clear?* Ask students for suggestions, and write their suggestions on the chalkboard. Here is one possible rewrite: *After I revised the order, a power outage knocked out the phones.*

✎ Write the following sentences on the chalkboard. Ask students to identify the dangling modifiers and revise the sentences to make their meanings clear.

1. Before picking up the supplies, the office must be notified. (I notified the office before picking up the supplies.)

2. After placing an ad, the warehouse hired three assistant managers. (After placing an ad, the senior warehouse manager hired three assistant managers.)

3. Before issuing the recommendations, the office staff read the manager's proposals. (John, Mark, and Mimi read the proposals before issuing the recommendations.)

4. Working around the clock to finish, the final report was impressive and on time. (Working around the clock to finish, Danny completed the report.)

5. After finishing the paperwork, reports need to be compiled. (After finishing the paperwork, Andy compiled the reports.)

Proofreading the Draft

Student Edition, pages 96–99

LEARNING OBJECTIVE

▶ Students will learn how to proofread a draft.

Lesson Resources

On the *CD-ROM*

- Topic at-a-Glance: Proofreading the Draft
- Application: Proofreading the Draft

In the *Handbook*

- Strategies for Proofreading Your Writing: 341–342
- Proofreading Checklist: 343

Additional Resources
From Globe Fearon:

- *Globe Exercise Books*
  Punctuation: 4–9, 22–23, 32–37
  Sentences: 26–33

- *Success in Writing*
  Writing to Explain: 36
  Grammar Skills for Writers: 66–82, 110–111
  Writing to Persuade: 36

- *Writer's Toolkit*
  Handbook: Grammar Handbook: Capitalization and Punctuation

INTO

Using Prior Knowledge

Once students have edited their drafts for content, the next step is to proofread. Proofreading allows students to correct punctuation errors that they might have missed. Ask students to brainstorm examples that show the difference between editing and proofreading. Ask students to preview the lesson headings and captions and predict what they will learn about proofreading the draft.

THROUGH

Developing the Lesson

Proofreading is an essential part of writing, but checking for all types of errors at once can seem overwhelming.

Discussing Visuals Review Figure 5-7 and Figure 5-8 on pages 97 and 98 of the Student Edition. Ask students to compile a proofreading checklist from the information in these two figures. Their checklist should include grammatical and proofreading points that they should check whenever they proofread. Ask students to use their checklists to proofread their Career reports.

BEYOND

Closing the Lesson

Ask students to use the proofreading checklist they developed to proofread the paragraph in the *Apply What You Learn* activity. Did they cover each item? Then, ask students to list the revisions they made to the paragraph and explain how they corrected the errors. Was a period missing from the end of a sentence? Did a verb agree with its subject?

ESL/LEP Tip

Students learning English may find that they make errors in usage because they are using different rules in English than they use in their native language. For example, students may need to eliminate sentence fragments or run-on sentences from their writing. Suggest that students remain aware of these errors and add them to the proofreading checklists they create. Next to each error, ask students to write a solution for correcting the error.

Curriculum Connection: Science

Ask students to imagine that they are being asked to conduct a lab experiment and have been given a list of materials. Tell students that the procedure should have specified 2 grams of magnesium instead of 20 grams of manganese. As a result, the experiment does not work. Ask students to think about the kind of information that can be affected if directions are not proofread.

TIP

Remind students that proper nouns and adjectives name a particular person, place, thing, or idea and that all of them need to be capitalized. Give students an example for each category:

- Person: *Sally Deptford*
- Place: *London*
- Thing: *Emancipation Proclamation*
- Idea: *Impressionism*

Lesson Resources

On the *CD-ROM*

- Grammar Workshop Practice: Using Capitalization Correctly
- Grammar Workshop Test: Using Capitalization Correctly
- Handbook Practice: Capitalization

In the *Handbook*

- Capitalization: 364

Additional Resources From Globe Fearon:

- *Globe Exercise Books* *Punctuation*: 32–39
- *Success in Writing* *Grammar Skills for Writers*: 66–67
- *Writer's Toolkit* Handbook: Grammar Handbook: Capitalization

USING CAPITALIZATION CORRECTLY

Grammar Workshop at-a-Glance

This Grammar Workshop identifies grammatical rules that govern capitalization. The lesson covers capitalization of the first words in sentences; first-person pronouns; proper nouns and adjectives; geographic areas, monuments, and well-known places; titles that precede names; and nationalities, languages, and religions.

Error Alert: Solving the Problem

- Draw a grid on the chalkboard. Give each of the following categories a box drawn down the left side of the grid: proper nouns, proper adjectives, geographic areas, monuments, titles, nationalities, languages, and religions.

- Ask students to suggest examples of things that should be capitalized.

  Some possible responses include

	Example 1	*Example 2*	*Example 3*
Proper nouns	James Madison	Alice Walker	Marie Curie
Proper adjectives	Italian bread	French dressing	English muffins
Geographic areas	San Francisco	Africa	Europe
Monuments	Eiffel Tower	Tower of Pisa	Taj Mahal
Titles	Mr. Green	Dr. Kaye	Monsignor Blake
Nationalities	American	Chinese	Indian
Languages	Swahili	Hindi	Arabic
Religions	Buddhist	Protestant	Jewish

Publishing a Document

Student Edition, pages 101–102

LEARNING OBJECTIVE

▶ Students will learn how to prepare a final document for publishing.

Lesson Resource

On the *CD-ROM*

• Topic at-a-Glance: Publishing a Document

INTO

Using Prior Knowledge

Bring to class a selection of different types of printed material, such as a memo, a letter, or a glossy brochure. Ask students to think about the look of each published piece of writing. How do audience and purpose influence final form? Ask students to preview the lesson headings and captions and predict what they will learn about publishing a document.

THROUGH

Developing the Lesson

In this lesson, students consider the format in which to publish their documents. Illustrate how business writing uses graphics and different formats by showing the examples of business writing that you brought to class. Ask students to select one of the examples. Working in groups, ask students to record three ways that the sample is successful and three ways to improve it. The analysis should address graphics, the format, and how well the piece addresses its intended audience and purpose.

Discussing Visuals Review Figure 5-10, *Writing in the Real World: The Published Document*, on page 102 of the Student Edition. Would Kendra's published document be as effective without the graphics? Ask students to explain why or why not.

BEYOND

Closing the Lesson

Ask the groups to complete the *Apply What You Learn* activity. Ask each group to suggest an alternative presentation for Kendra's piece using a different format and graphics. When the groups have finished, have them present their analyses and alternative designs to the class.

ESL/LEP Tip

Familiarize students with the different kinds of graphics their textbooks and certain magazines and newspapers use. Ask students if these graphics make the final product attractive to the reader. Do these make the information in the final product easier to understand?

Job Path Project

Students' reports on career choices should now be complete. Ask each student to consider how he or she might want to publish the report. Encourage students to be creative. For example, students may want to make a brochure designed to inform classmates of career opportunities in a field. Allow students time in class to present oral summaries of their work and to display their published versions.

Additional Resources
From Globe Fearon:

• *Success in Writing*
  Writing to Describe: 36
  Writing to Explain: 37
  Writing to Persuade: 37

Creating Word-Processing Documents
(Student Edition, page 81)

Virtually every student will have to prepare a document using word processing in his or her career. This is a skill that many employers require of entry-level employees. You might consider asking your students to write a report using a word-processing program. Tell students who do not have access to word processors at school or home that many libraries have computers that they can use. Tell students that tutorials are available online for those who need help with word processing. One good source of help is this Website: www.vwc.edu/library_tech/tutorials/word.html

Saving Documents
(Student Edition, page 103)

Explain to students that saving a document is an important word-processing skill. Point out that students should save their documents as a precaution before printing. Explain that they should consider saving important work on both the hard drive and a floppy disk. Demonstrate how to automatically save text at specified intervals, such as every ten minutes. Then, ask students to practice saving their own documents.

Additional Resource
From Globe Fearon:

*Survival Guide for
Computer Literacy*: 60

UNIT 3

WRITING TO EXPLAIN

Student Edition, page 107

CAREER FILE PROJECT SUPPORT

On page 144 of the Student Edition, students will read about cashiers and restaurant managers. Explain that each of these positions requires interaction with the public. Ask students if they have ever worked with the public. What kinds of situations did they encounter? How did they deal with them? Tell students who are interested in either of these careers to arrange a job-shadowing opportunity. Students can record their experiences using the job-shadowing application on the CD-ROM.

Action Profile

Ask students to choose one of the two careers profiled in this unit and answer the following questions:

1. What type of experience, education, and training do employers expect of those they hire?
2. Are there any local or state requirements for working in this field?
3. What interests and traits do you have that would make this a good job for you?
4. Does the job have any requirements you may have difficulty meeting?
5. What related fields may interest you?

Because of the importance of explanatory writing in business and in life, this unit is devoted to helping students understand how to speak and write to explain. These pages provide a range of strategies for giving students practice with this important skill.

What's in the Unit

In this unit, students learn how to write, follow, and give directions. They also learn how to read and understand the steps of a process and how to write these steps clearly and completely.

Previewing the Unit

Every student has had experience giving directions. Ask students to describe written and oral directions they have given and received. Encourage them to explain why some directions are clear while others can be difficult to follow. Were the words confusing? Were the directions out of order? Ask students to preview the unit by looking at the titles, headings, subheadings, figures, photos, illustrations, captions, and key words. Then, ask them to predict what they will learn in this unit. What kinds of processes can directions be used to explain?

Developing the Unit

As you begin work on this unit, ask students to bring to class examples of both helpful and unhelpful directions and explanations. A good source for examples is the explanatory material that comes with electronic equipment or furniture that requires assembly. Ask students to put the examples of useful directions in one pile and the examples of less successful directions in another pile. Ask students to analyze what makes directions useful and what makes them less successful.

ACTIVITY	MINUTES
Preview lesson headings, captions, and boldfaced words; five-minute free-write on how students plan and execute major writing assignments	10
Read and discuss Lessons 6–1 and 6–2	20
Small groups meet to discuss *Apply What You Learn*, Lesson 6-1	10
Writing: Sample directions for using equipment or doing a particular task	20
Discuss Workplace Workshop: Correcting Run-on Sentences	15
Small groups meet to discuss *Apply What You Learn*, Lesson 6-2	10
Concluding reflections, assignments, answer questions	5

IN-DEPTH DISCOVERY

Resources for students to explore include

- *How to Write Policies, Procedures & Task Outlines: Sending Clear Signals in Written Directions* by Larry Peabody and John Gear. Ravensdale, WA: Idyll Arbor, 1998. A manual to help readers organize, separate, and format policies, procedures and tasks.

- *Writing Effective Policies and Procedures: A Step-By-Step Resource for Clear Communication* by Nancy Campbell. New York: AMACOM, 1998. This book provides helpful guidelines and background material to design procedures.

- *Establishing a System of Policies and Procedures* by Steve Page. Mansfield, OH: Bookmasters, 1998. A step-by-step explanation of how to write procedures correctly.

Within the Family

Illustrate the difficulty of giving clear directions by asking students to give a family member directions for a simple household task, such as making a sandwich or taking out the trash. Ask students to report on their results to the class. How successfully did family members accomplish the tasks? Did family members have trouble successfully completing the tasks? Why?

Job Path Project

Ask students to continue doing research on their careers of choice. Ask each student to find a person who works in that career and to arrange to shadow that person on the job. Students can record their experiences using the job-shadowing application on the CD-ROM. During their visits, ask students to look for examples of how explanatory and process writing is used in the workplace. Were directions for using office equipment posted? Were graphics used to show a process?

Discussing the Quote

Ask students to read the quote by Maria Goeppert-Mayer on page 107 of the Student Edition. What might Maria Goeppert-Mayer say about writing to explain a process?

Closing the Unit

Test students' ability to write a one-page explanation of how to get from their classroom to the cafeteria. Then, ask them to exchange papers and write a critique of one another's writing for clarity and effectiveness. Were these directions accurate? inaccurate? What made them useful? What would make them more useful? As students complete each chapter in this unit, you can use the chapter assessments located on the CD-ROM to check their progress.

CHAPTER **6**	

Student Edition, pages 108–109

READING AND WRITING DIRECTIONS
English in Context

TEACHING THE CHAPTER OPENER

Monica, a cashier at a supermarket, has been asked by the store manager to explain her job to a new employee. Monica knows her job well, but the prospect of explaining everything that a cashier needs to know overwhelms her. Monica needs to learn how to give directions effectively.

• Ask students to give Monica advice that will help her prepare a thorough explanation for Simon. What should Monica keep in mind when preparing her explanation? Ask students to list their suggestions for Monica.

PORTFOLIO SETUP: WRITING INSTRUCTIONS

• On page 121 of the Student Edition, students are asked to write a set of instructions. Ask students to brainstorm different workplace tasks. Some of these tasks could include keeping records of a sale, handling a complaint, or performing a specific operation on a computer. Ask students to give instructions for a workplace task in the form of a memo or an e-mail. Make peer-editing a part of this assignment and refer students to the proofreading checklist they developed in Chapter 5.

CD-ROM TEAMWORK/COOPERATIVE ACTIVITY

• In this activity, groups of three or four students take turns giving directions for completing a complicated skill, while the other students critique the presentation. The Teamwork/Cooperative Activity on the CD-ROM also contains a set of questions students can use to assess one another's performance.

LESSON PLANNING CHART

CHAPTER 6	STUDENT EDITION PAGES	TEACHER'S RESOURCE MANUAL PAGES	CD-ROM
Writing/Reading Activities	111, 113, 114, 117–121	46, 48, 49, 51	✓
Speaking/Listening Activities	111, 113, 117, 121	46, 48, 50	✓
Career Activities	117, 121		✓
Critical Thinking Activities	110–112, 115, 120, 121	46, 47	✓
Vocabulary Activities	109, 120	50	✓
ESL/LEP Tips		47, 50	
Teamwork/Cooperative Activities	113, 121	46, 48, 50	✓
Curriculum Connections		47, 48	
Technology Activities	119	50, 60	

Reading and Following Directions

Student Edition, pages 110–111

LEARNING OBJECTIVE

▶ Students will learn how to interpret oral and written directions.

Lesson Resources

On the *CD-ROM*

• Application: Reading and Following Directions

In the *Handbook*

• Reading Strategies: 332–336

INTO

Using Prior Knowledge

Ask students if they have heard of products for which, "Assembly is required." What does this term mean? Ask students if they have ever purchased an item that requires assembly. Were the directions clear and easy to follow? Were there any diagrams? Ask students to preview the lesson headings and captions and predict what they will learn about reading and following directions.

THROUGH

Developing the Lesson

The lesson offers guidelines for listening to directions, such as using word clues, and it offers strategies for reading directions, such as looking for key words in each step.

Discussing Visuals Review Figure 6-1 on page 111 of the Student Edition. How useful are these directions? Ask students to label the set of directions in Figure 6-1 using these strategies. If the students find problems with the directions, they should also label these. Ask students to draft a solution to any problem they discover. Have groups present their analyses to the class.

BEYOND

Closing the Lesson

After students have completed the *Apply What You Learn* activity and have exchanged papers with one another, ask them to make concrete suggestions for improving each other's directions. Can the directions be made any clearer? Are any steps missing? Ask students to refer to the strategies for reading directions on page 111 of the Student Edition.

ESL/LEP Tip

Ask students learning English to bring in photocopied directions or instructions that they found frustrating. Ask them to underline the confusing words or sentences. Ask an English-proficient student to work with the students to explain the underlined sections and write a clearer version of the directions.

Curriculum Connection: Science

Ask students to bring in directions for a science experiment they have conducted. Have students photocopy the directions, underline the words that illustrate the reading strategies discussed on page 111 of the Student Edition, and write, in their own words, how they would perform the experiment.

Additional Resource
From Globe Fearon:

• *Success in Writing*
Writing to Explain: 47–53

Giving Directions
Student Edition, pages 112–113

LEARNING OBJECTIVES

▶ Students will learn how to provide accurate oral and written directions.

▶ Students will acquire and use feedback.

Lesson Resource

On the *CD-ROM*

• Teamwork/Cooperative Activity: Giving Directions

INTO
Using Prior Knowledge

Demonstrate the importance of giving clear directions by giving unclear ones for a simple activity. For example, ask each student to take out a sheet of paper and write his or her name on it without specifying where on the page. Then, ask students to give you the papers without specifying whether they should pass them to the front or hand them to you. Give the instructions in the wrong order, backtrack, and contradict yourself. Explain that you have just provided an example of the importance of providing clear directions. Then, ask students to preview the lesson headings and captions and predict what they will learn about giving directions.

THROUGH
Developing the Lesson

Lesson 6-2 on pages 112–113 of the Student Edition outlines the steps for giving clear directions. These steps include identifying audience and purpose, making a plan, using effective methods to help create directions, and asking for feedback. Review the lesson under each heading. Why is brainstorming important? What are some tips for giving directions? Why is feedback important? After students read the lesson, they can choose either a procedure or a piece of equipment and use the tips and guidelines on pages 112–113 of the Student Edition to write directions. When students are done, they can trade directions with one another and get feedback on the effectiveness of their writing.

BEYOND
Closing the Lesson

Ask students to complete the *Apply What You Learn* activity by working in pairs to rewrite directions that students found hard to understand. Was any part of the directions misleading? incomplete? unclear? Tell students to use the tips and guidelines on pages 112–113 of the Student Edition.

Curriculum Connection: Art

Bring to class various photographs and illustrations from books and magazines. Ask students to choose one of the photographs or illustrations. Tell students to pair up and sit opposite each other. Then, ask one student to describe his or her photograph or illustration and the other student to draw what his or her partner is describing. Does the student's drawing resemble the photograph or illustration his or her partner described?

Additional Resource
From Globe Fearon:

• *Success in Writing*
Writing to Explain: 47–53

Grammar Workshop

TIP

The key to correcting run-on sentences is recognizing when there is more than one complete thought in a sentence. Tell your students that when they find a long sentence that has more than one complete thought, these thoughts need to be separated.

Lesson Resources

On the *CD-ROM*

- Grammar Workshop Practice: Correcting Run-on Sentences
- Grammar Workshop Test: Correcting Run-on Sentences
- Handbook Practice: Simple, Compound, and Complex Sentences

In the *Handbook*

- Sentences: 346

Additional Resources From Globe Fearon:

- *Globe Exercise Books* *Sentences*: 32–33

- *Success in Writing* *Grammar Skills for Writers*: 20

- *Writer's Toolkit* Handbook: Problem Solver: Correcting Run-On Sentences

CORRECTING RUN-ON SENTENCES

Grammar Workshop at-a-Glance

In this Grammar Workshop, students learn three ways to correct run-on sentences: using an end punctuation mark, using a comma and connecting words, and using a semicolon to separate two complete thoughts.

Error Alert: Solving the Problem

- Write this sentence on the chalkboard: *We ran out of copier paper we ordered more.*

- Ask students, *Is this sentence correct*? (no; two sentences written as one long sentence.)

- Ask students, *What are the two different, complete thoughts in this sentence*? (We ran out of copier paper, and we ordered more.) *How can we separate these two complete thoughts using a period*? (We ran out of copier paper. We ordered more.)

- Ask students, *How can we use a comma and a connecting word to connect these two complete thoughts*? (We ran out of copier paper, so we ordered more.) *What are some other examples of connecting words*? (and, but, for, nor, or, yet)

- Ask students, *How can we use a semicolon to separate these two complete thoughts*? (We ran out of copier paper; we ordered more.)

Write the following sentences on the chalkboard. Ask students to rewrite each of the following sentences using each of the three methods shown above.

1. Jill carefully opened the box she told her colleagues the supplies arrived.

2. I finished my report I left it in my office.

3. Alan and Dara had an important meeting they left early.

4. Shanti got a new job she is eager to start working.

5. Our presentation was really successful everyone loved it.

Ways to Communicate

Student Edition, pages 115–117

LEARNING OBJECTIVE

▶ Students will use writing techniques to compose memos and e-mail.

INTO
Using Prior Knowledge

Ask students how they communicate with their friends. Do they call them on the phone? send a letter? send an e-mail? Does the information they want to communicate determine the format they choose? Ask students how their phone conversations, letters, or e-mail would be different if they were writing to a teacher or prospective employer. Ask students to preview the lesson headings and captions and predict what they will learn about ways to communicate.

THROUGH
Developing the Lesson

Lesson 6-3 on pages 115–117 of the Student Edition focuses on signs, posters, memoranda, and e-mail as different ways to communicate. Students learn about these different formats and when each is appropriate for business communications.

Discussing Visuals Review Figures 6-3 and 6-4, *Writing in the Real World: Memo*, on pages 115 and 116 of the Student Edition. How do these types of formats differ from one another? Which kind of information is best communicated using a sign or poster? a memorandum? an e-mail?

BEYOND
Closing the Lesson

Students can work in pairs to complete the *Apply What You Learn* activity. Ask them to exchange their finished work with other pairs for peer editing. Then, ask students to imagine that they work in an office. Ask students to rewrite the information for senior staff members who will be coming from another office. Ask students to consider the change in audience. Should students use the same format?

ESL/LEP Tip

Students may have difficulties with some of the vocabulary in this lesson, such as *memo* and *e-mail*. Help students understand the meanings of these words and what they are by telling them that *memo* is short for *memorandum* and that *e-mail* is short for *electronic mail*.

Web Activity

Visit www.colostate.edu/depts/WritingCenter with your students. This site helps students learn about writing and researching. The Writing and Teaching Guide provides many links that have information on specific topics, such as e-mail and memos.

Additional Resources
From Globe Fearon:

• *Writer's Toolkit*
  Drafting: *Memo Shell*

• *Survival Guide for
  Computer Literacy:*
  107

Grammar Workshop

CHANGING PASSIVE VOICE TO ACTIVE VOICE

Grammar Workshop at-a-Glance

In this *Grammar Workshop*, students learn that the voice of a verb shows whether the subject performs or receives the action of the verb. Students also learn how to change a passive voice to an active voice.

Error Alert: Solving the Problem

- Write these two sentences on the chalkboard: (1) *The analysis was made by him.* (2) *He made the analysis.*

- Ask students, *Which one of these sentences is clearer?* (the second one)

- Tell students, *The second version sounds better, because the subject is performing the action. This makes the subject active, so the sentence is written in the active voice.*

- Ask students, *Is the subject in Sentence 1 performing or receiving the action?* (receiving)

- Ask students, *Because the subject of the sentence,* the analysis, *is receiving the action, this sentence is written in the passive voice.*

- Write this sentence on the chalkboard: *A design was created for the new office by Jilani.*

- *How could we rewrite the sentence so that the person, or thing, performing the action is the subject of the sentence? First, let's look at who is performing the action.* (Jilani) *Because he is performing the action, we want to change* Jilani, *from a receiver* (passive) *to a doer* (active). (Jilani created the design.) *Think of this sentence as an example of the performer of the action taking an active role in the action.*

- Write these sentences on the chalkboard. Then, ask students to rewrite each sentence so that it is in the active voice.

  1. The task was performed by Jake. (Jake performed the task.)

  2. The door was closed by Jean. (Jean closed the door.)

  3. The tax preparer was told to complete her work. (I told the tax preparer to complete her work.)

  4. The lessons were learned. (Everyone learned the lessons.)

  5. The news was learned late yesterday. (We learned the news late yesterday.)

TIP

Explain that the active voice makes a connection between the person or thing and what is being done. Tell students that they should use the active voice in their writing and that the person or thing that performs the action should be the subject of the sentence.

Lesson Resources

On the *CD-ROM*

- Grammar Workshop Practice: Changing Passive Voice to Active Voice
- Grammar Workshop Test: Changing Passive Voice to Active Voice
- Handbook Practice: Active and Passive Voice

In the *Handbook*

- Voice: 352

Additional Resource From Globe Fearon:

- *Success in Writing Grammar Skills for Writers*: 91

Student Edition, pages 122–123

WRITING TO EXPLAIN A PROCESS
English in Context

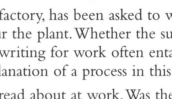

TEACHING THE CHAPTER OPENER

Roberto, who works in the office of a luggage-manufacturing factory, has been asked to write an explanation of the luggage-making process for visitors who tour the plant. Whether the subject is making luggage or dealing with closing a store at the end of a day, writing for work often entails writing about processes. Students will learn the steps to writing an explanation of a process in this chapter.

• Ask students who have had jobs to recall processes they have read about at work. Was there a sign near the photocopying machine that explained how to use the machine?

PORTFOLIO SETUP: WRITING AN EXPLANATION

• On page 143 of the Student Edition, students are asked to write an explanation. Ask students to brainstorm a list of work processes. Then, ask them to work in small groups and choose one of the processes. Ask students to share their ideas before they write their explanations. Have groups reconvene so students can read and edit one another's work and discuss the use of graphics.

CD-ROM TEAMWORK/COOPERATIVE ACTIVITY

• This exercise gives groups experience in creating charts, graphs, and tables. Groups either choose one of the suggested ideas or come up with their own, and then they produce the graphics.

LESSON PLANNING CHART			
CHAPTER 7	STUDENT EDITION PAGES	TEACHER'S RESOURCE MANUAL PAGES	CD-ROM
Writing/Reading Activities	126, 128, 132, 133, 140, 142–144	52, 54, 56,57, 59	✓
Speaking/Listening Activities	128, 132, 139, 142, 143	52, 55, 57	✓
Career Activities	143, 144	54	✓
Critical Thinking Activities	124, 127, 129, 132, 134, 136, 137, 142–144	52–55, 57, 58	✓
Vocabulary Activities	123, 142		✓
ESL/LEP Tips		53, 55	
Teamwork/Cooperative Activities	128, 139	52, 55, 57	✓
Curriculum Connections		58	
Technology Activities	141	55, 60	✓

Reading an Explanation of a Process

Student Edition, pages 124–126

LEARNING OBJECTIVE

▶ Students will understand the steps of the writing process.

Lesson Resource

📖 **In the Handbook**

• Reading Strategies: 332–336

INTO

Using Prior Knowledge

Reading an explanation of a process is easiest when the explanation is presented in clear, concise steps. Ask students how they break apart an explanation when they have to explain a process. What kinds of information do they include? Ask students to think about explanations they have read. What made these explanations easy to read and understand? Then, ask students to preview the lesson headings and captions and predict what they will learn about reading an explanation of a process.

THROUGH

Developing the Lesson

Students learn how to identify writing that explains a process by recognizing the specific structure it follows. They learn that they will encounter writing that explains a process at school, at home, and at work. Discuss the types of such writing that students read at school, at home, and at work. How are they the same? How are they different? Students also learn the steps of a reading strategy that can help them successfully and carefully read explanations: preview, read, write, and review.

Discussing Visuals Review Figures 7-1 and 7-2 on pages 124 and 125 of the Student Edition. What characteristics allow students to identify these as examples of writing that explains a process? Review each of the steps of the reading strategy outlined in Figure 7-3 on page 126 of the Student Edition. Then, ask students to use these steps as a strategy for reading the examples of writing in Figures 7-1 and 7-2. How did the four-step strategy help students understand the explanation of how an ATM works?

BEYOND

Closing the Lesson

Ask students to refer to the writing they used for the *Apply What You Learn* activity. Ask students to review the explanation using the four steps of the reading strategy in Figure 7-3 on page 126 of the Student Edition. Ask students to explain how this strategy helps them understand the explanation.

ESL/LEP Tip

Make sure that students understand the terminology used in the four-step strategy. Ask English-proficient students to define each of the steps for students. Then, ask English-proficient students to help students model the four steps.

Additional Resources From Globe Fearon:

• *Globe Exercise Books*
  Paragraphs: 38

• *Writer's Toolkit*
  Modes: Exposition

Gathering Information

Student Edition, pages 127–128

LEARNING OBJECTIVE

▶ Students will learn how to collect information about a process.

Lesson Resource

On the *CD-ROM*

- Topic at-a-Glance:
  Gathering Information

INTO

Using Prior Knowledge

Gathering information is an important step before writing about a process or writing a report. Ask students to think about how they gather information before they write. Ask a volunteer to explain how he or she gathered information for a recent report. Then, ask students to preview the lesson headings and captions and predict what they will learn about gathering information.

THROUGH

Developing the Lesson

Students reading this lesson will learn how to gather information to write an explanation of a process. They will learn to think about the purpose and the audience for this type of writing. They will also learn to look at different sources, such as library resources, electronic resources, personal observations, and interviews. Ask students to write down the different sources discussed on pages 127 and 128 of the Student Edition. For what kind of report would library resources be useful? personal observations? interviews? Ask students to work in pairs and think of a process they would like to describe, such as playing a game, cooking dinner, or opening a checking account. Be certain that the subject is one that students will have to research to explain. Then, have students compile a list of sources and explain what kind of information each source provided them

BEYOND

Closing the Lesson

Ask each pair to look at the explanations from the *Apply What You Learn* activity. Then, ask them to consider the kinds of sources that the writers consulted when they prepared each of the pieces. Are there testimonials? Did the writers provide Web addresses?

Extending the Lesson

Ask students to find explanations of processes that are either well or poorly written. Then, ask them to choose one example and rewrite it so that it is clear and complete. What did they change to make their version clearer?

Job Path Project

Ask students to review what they learned about the career they are researching. Ask them to identify a process that someone in that field might need to complete. Ask students to consider the audience, research the process, and suggest sources of information.

Additional Resources
From Globe Fearon:

- *Success in Writing*
  Writing to Explain: 25

- *Writer's Toolkit*
  Gathering Details

Writing an Explanation
Student Edition, pages 129–132

LEARNING OBJECTIVES

◗ Students will learn how to sort and organize information about a process.

◗ Students will learn how to write a clear, concise explanation.

Lesson Resources

On the *CD-ROM*
- Various graphic organizers

In the *Handbook*
- The Writing Process: 337
- Strategies for Organizing Your Writing: 338–339

Additional Resources From Globe Fearon:

- *Globe Exercise Books*
  Paragraphs: 16–19, 24–25

- *Success in Writing*
  Writing to Explain: 20–22, 28–32

- *Writer's Toolkit*
  Choosing a Topic: Timeline; Revising and Editing: Unity and Coherence Check

INTO

Using Prior Knowledge

Writing an explanation requires the writer to be clear and concise. To demonstrate the difficulty of writing an explanation, ask students to do a free-write in which they explain how to tie their shoes. Tell them that the explanation must be understandable to someone who has never seen a pair of shoelaces before. When students are done, discuss the difficulties of writing an explanation of a process. Ask students to preview the lesson headings and captions and predict what they will learn about writing an explanation.

THROUGH

Developing the Lesson

This lesson discusses the steps of writing an explanation: planning the explanation, limiting the topic, organizing the information, and writing the first draft. Point out to students that these are the same steps they use in other kinds of writing.

Discussing Visuals Review Figure 7-5, *Writing in the Real World: Explanation of a Process*, on page 131 of the Student Edition. Discuss how the different steps of the process are represented in the explanation of how a mouse works. Did the writer plan the explanation well? limit the topic? organize the information? compile all the information into a concise draft? How can you tell?

BEYOND

Closing the Lesson

Ask students to complete the *Apply What You Learn* activity independently. Then, ask students to form small groups and discuss the general quality of the process explanations they analyzed. Did the writer limit the topic? organize the information? compile all the information into a concise draft? How can you tell?

ESL/LEP Tip

Writing about processes can include jargon and unusual words that students are unfamiliar with. Ask an English-proficient student to help define the confusing words. Have the students add the words to their personal dictionaries.

Web Activity

Ask students to brainstorm topics that explain a process. These can include preparing a recipe, resolving a conflict, or conducting a science experiment. Ask students to search www.nytimes.com/learning to find an article that explains a process. Did the writer plan the explanation well? limit the topic? organize the information? compile all the information into a concise draft? How can you tell?

Grammar Workshop

Student Edition, page 133

MAKING PRONOUNS AND THEIR ANTECEDENTS AGREE

Grammar Workshop at-a-Glance

Grammar Workshop shows students how to make certain that the pronouns they use agree with their antecedents. Students will learn how to match pronouns by number, gender, and person.

Error Alert: Solving the Problem

Write this sentence on the chalkboard: *Jen found her lost papers.*

- Ask students, *First, let's find the pronoun. What is the pronoun in this sentence?* (her) *Let's circle the antecedent,* Jen, *and the pronoun,* her. *Now, let's draw a line from one circle to the other.*

- Tell students, *There are three things to look for when making pronouns agree with their antecedents: agreement in number, gender, and person.*

- *Let's check for agreement in number. How many Jens are there?* (one) *Does the antecedent* Jen *agree with the pronoun* her *in number?* (yes)

- *Let's check for agreement in gender. Is* Jen *male or female?* (female) *Does the antecedent* Jen *agree with the pronoun* her *in gender?* (yes)

- *Let's check for agreement in person. If the antecedent is first person, the word would be* I. *If the antecedent is second person, the word would be* you. *If the antecedent is being spoken about, it is third person. Is* Jen *first, second, or third person?* (third) *Does the antecedent* Jen *agree with the pronoun* her *in person?* (yes)

 Write the following sentences on the chalkboard. Ask students to make a chart and identify the number, gender, and person for each sentence. Then, ask them to explain what the error is and what the correct word should be.

1. Bob had her interview. (his)

2. He doesn't know their Social Security number. (his)

3. Rasheed and I finished my work. (our)

4. Women who take that job will need his wits about him. (their, them)

5. The copying machine quit doing his job. (its)

Using Precise Details

Student Edition, pages 134–136

LEARNING OBJECTIVE

▶ Students will learn how to use precise details when they write.

Lesson Resources

On the *CD-ROM*

• Topic at-a-Glance: Using Precise Details

• Application: Using Precise Details

Additional Resources
From Globe Fearon:

• *Globe Exercise Books*
  Mechanics and Usage: 38–39
  Sentences: 36–37
  Spelling and Vocabulary: 40–43

• *Success in Writing*
  Writing to Describe: 49
  Grammar Skills for Writers: 22–23

• *Writer's Toolkit*
  Writing Handbook: Elements of Writing: Choosing Words

• *Be a Better Reader*
  Level G: 94

INTO
Using Prior Knowledge

Write this sentence on the chalkboard: *Attach it over there.* Ask students if they know what the sentence is telling them to do. Explain that what is needed are precise details that tell what *it* is and where *over there* is. Ask students to preview the lesson headings and captions and predict what they will learn about using precise details.

THROUGH
Developing the Lesson

This lesson explains how to choose precise details to express ideas as well as the transition words that help students clarify these ideas. Students learn how to use a dictionary and a thesaurus to correct poor word choice. Explain that the incorrect use of vocabulary can affect meaning and accuracy as much as the use of inaccurate details. Review each of the headings with the students. Ask students to give additional examples that illustrate each of the main points. For example, ask students to talk about the connotation of the words *slender* and *skinny*. Then, ask students to name other words with positive and negative connotations. Ask students to bring in a recent piece of writing that contains details. Ask students to exchange papers and edit them for precise details and word choice. Are the words used specific? Is the paper too wordy? Are the connections between ideas clear?

BEYOND
Closing the Lesson

After students complete the *Apply What You Learn* activity, ask them to copy only the details of the process onto a separate sheet of paper. Ask students to exchange papers with each other. Then, ask them to identify the process on the basis of the details alone. If students guessed the process right away, what made it easy to identify? If students had difficulty recognizing the process, what might have made it easier to identify?

Job Path Project

By now, students will have a considerable body of written work in their Career Folders. Ask them to review what they have written and check for precise details. Tell students to check a dictionary to confirm the precise meaning of words they have used, and tell them to use a thesaurus to find synonyms to vary their word choice. Is the paper too wordy? Are the connections between ideas clear?

Using Graphics to Explain a Process

Student Edition, pages 137–139

INTO

Using Prior Knowledge

Charts, graphs, or other visuals can give readers a clear picture of what the writer is trying to communicate. Discuss the statement "A picture is worth a thousand words" with students. You may also consider finding two books that illustrate different approaches to graphics. The graphics in one book should be difficult to understand. The graphics in the second book should help the reader understand the book's content. Encourage students to point out the differences between the graphics. Then, ask students to preview the lesson headings and captions and predict what they will learn about using graphics to explain a process.

THROUGH

Developing the Lesson

On pages 137–139 of the Student Edition, students learn about the benefits of using visuals, such as drawings, photographs, charts, graphs, maps, and diagrams, to explain a process. They learn the best way to use charts, tables, graphs, and diagrams to complement their text.

Discussing Visuals Review Figures 7-6 through 7-10 on pages 137–139 of the Student Edition with students. What makes these visuals useful? Ask students to work in pairs and imagine they are working on a company's annual report. Ask students to create graphics that explain, month-by-month, how many products the company sold in one year. What kinds of labels should students include to make their graphics clear?

BEYOND

Closing the Lesson

Ask students to review Figures 7-6 through 7-10. Which is the easiest to understand? Why? Ask the class to brainstorm both a list of the characteristics that make graphics effective and a list of things to avoid when using graphics in writing. Write student suggestions on the chalkboard, and discuss each list.

Curriculum Connection: Social Studies

Ask students to look at magazines and find a graph, table, or chart that provides information about economics, geography, demographics, and so on. Ask students to explain how the graph, table, or chart they selected relays information to readers.

LEARNING OBJECTIVE

▶ Students will learn to use graphics to explain a process.

Lesson Resources

On the *CD-ROM*

- Topic at-a-Glance: Using Graphics to Explain a Process
- Application: Using Graphics to Explain a Process
- Teamwork/Cooperative Activity: Creating Graphics

USING COMMAS TO CLARIFY

Grammar Workshop at-a-Glance

This Grammar Workshop explains how to use commas to separate words, phrases, or clauses in a series; to separate a noun of address from the rest of the sentence; and to set off a word, phrase, or clause that disturbs the flow of a sentence.

Error Alert: Solving the Problem

Write this sentence on the chalkboard: *I went to the store bought some groceries drove home and then cooked dinner.*

- Ask students, *Where do the commas belong in this sentence?* (I went to the store, bought some groceries, drove home, and then cooked dinner.)

- Write this sentence on the chalkboard: *You did a wonderful job on the presentation Mike.*

- Ask students, *Who is being addressed in this sentence?* (Mike) Ask students, *Where does the comma belong in this sentence?* (You did a wonderful job on the presentation, Mike.)

- Write this sentence on the chalkboard: *Mariel my friend and colleague is a very talented architect.*

- Ask students, *What word, phrase, or clause is interrupting the flow of the sentence?* (my friend and colleague) Ask students, *Where do the commas belong?* (Mariel, my friend and colleague, is a very talented architect.)

Write these sentences on the chalkboard. Ask students to correct each sentence by properly placing any missing commas.

1. Please proofread photocopy and staple the reports on my desk. (proofread, photocopy, and staple)

2. This magazine which is published four times a year has a lot of information about careers. (magazine, which is published four times a year, has)

3. Madeleine did you send the application to Mr. Johnson? (Madeleine,)

4. Our receptionist answers the phone types letters and files reports. (answers the phone, types letters, and)

5. Perry will you be leaving early staying late or taking tomorrow off? (Perry, will you be leaving early, staying late, or)

TECH CONNECTIONS

E-Mail
(Student Edition, page 119)

E-mail is a vital tool in today's business world. Tell students that they should always think carefully about the contents of an e-mail message, and they should always re-read an e-mail message before sending it. Explain that e-mail is a quick and easy way to communicate, so it is easy to make errors. Also, tell students that this is a written medium, and they should always be conscious of the way they communicate tone. Ask pairs of students to practice creating e-mail messages to send to each other. For example, they can send e-mail as an employer to an employee asking how to solve a problem, or as a salesperson to a prospective client asking if the client has any questions about a product.

Internet Resource Web Sites
(Student Edition, page 141)

Ask students to suppose they are researching a work of art in a museum or a famous building in a foreign country. How would they go about this research? Explain to students that resources, such as encyclopedias, dictionaries, almanacs, tutorials, and virtual museums are all available on the Internet. These resources make information gathering easy. Ask students how they use the Web as a resource for homework. How do they search? What techniques have they found most effective? Which sites are most helpful with social studies topics? Science topics? Math topics? Language arts topics? Why are each of these sites helpful?

Additional Resource
From Globe Fearon:

*Survival Guide for
Computer Literacy*: 100, 107

UNIT 4

WRITING REPORTS TO DESCRIBE AND PERSUADE

Student Edition, page 145

CAREER FILE PROJECT SUPPORT
On page 200 of the Student Edition, students will read about data entry clerks and paralegals. Anyone who enjoys working on the computer might enjoy being a data entry clerk. A paralegal is a perfect job for students who are intrigued by the law. Paralegals work closely with lawyers, and some eventually attend law school.

Action Profile
Ask students to choose one of the two careers profiled in this unit and answer the following questions:

1. What experience, education, and training do employers expect of those they hire?

2. Are there any local or state requirements for working in this field?

3. What interests and traits do you have that would make this a good job for you?

4. Does the job have any requirements you might have difficulty meeting?

5. What related fields might interest you?

All employees, from clerks to company presidents, find themselves writing reports that describe and persuade. These reports can range from sales reports to glossy, four-color annual reports. An employee who has the ability to write a report performs a valuable function for an employer and can open up opportunities for advancement. Unit 4 includes strategies that will help students learn to write to describe and persuade.

What's in the Unit

Chapter 8 addresses reading and writing formal and informal reports that describe. Students learn how to handle each stage of writing a long report—from prewriting to the final draft. Chapter 9 addresses reading and writing to persuade. Students learn persuasive writing techniques, as well as how to use graphics. Students also learn how to write a sales letter, advertising and catalog copy, and press releases.

Previewing the Unit

This unit will help students to learn the techniques that will enable them to write reports that describe and persuade. Ask students to preview the unit by looking at the titles, headings, subheadings, figures, photos, illustrations, captions, and key words. Then, ask them to predict what they will learn in this unit. How do words give a writer power?

Developing the Unit

As students read the unit, ask them to look for business writing that is persuasive and descriptive. Ask students to bring to class one example of each type of writing. Create a classroom portfolio of writing samples that students can refer to as they read the unit.

ACTIVITY	MINUTES
Preview lesson headings, captions, and boldfaced words; show examples of descriptive business writing	10
Read and discuss Lessons 8-1 and 8-2	20
Small groups meet to discuss *Apply What You Learn*, Lesson 8-1	10
Writing: Practice researching sources by *Apply What You Learn*, Lesson 8-2	20
Discuss Grammar Workshop: Practicing Word Choice	15
Small groups meet to discuss methods for collecting information	10
Concluding reflections, assignments, answer questions	5

IN-DEPTH DISCOVERY

Resources for students to explore include

- *The Elements of Style* by William Strunk Jr., et al. New York: Allyn & Bacon, 1999. This book explains the rules and guidelines for effective writing.

- *On Writing Well: The Classic Guide to Writing Nonfiction* by William Knowlton Zinsser. New York: Harperreference, 1998. This book gives advice on the basics of writing nonfiction.

- *Persuading on Paper: The Complete Guide to Writing Copy That Pulls in Business* by Marcia Yudkin. New York: Plume, 1996. This is a reference guide to effective written communication.

Within the Family

Interview family members about the kinds of descriptive and persuasive reports they have to write for their jobs. Examples include writing quarterly reports, job descriptions, and performance reviews. Ask students to write a paragraph that shows what they have learned.

Job Path Project

Students can use the information in this chapter to help them organize and write their Career reports. Students can also research and write a report about a business that is related to the careers that interest them. For example, if they are interested in health care, they can write a report exploring opportunities in physical therapy.

Discussing the Quote

Ask students to read the quote by Dean Rusk on page 145 of the Student Edition. How does this quote relate to writing to persuade?

Closing the Unit

Many libraries have annual reports from businesses and nonprofit groups, reports on the business page of a newspaper, press releases, and so on. Borrow these reports and have small groups of students analyze the writing. Students within each group can analyze a section of the report. They can begin by identifying the parts and organizational structure, listing the sources of information, and analyzing the writing. As your students complete each chapter in this unit, you can use the chapter assessments located on the CD-ROM to check their progress.

Student Edition, pages 146–147

WRITING REPORTS THAT DESCRIBE
English in Context

TEACHING THE CHAPTER OPENER

Yolanda has become head of the data-processing department at a catalog company. Her uncertainty about how to write a report is a problem. Students may think that report writing is a skill that only applies to school, but the ability to write well can lead to better jobs and better job performance. In this chapter, students will learn how to organize and write reports.

• Ask students what kind of reports they think they might write at work. Formal? informal?

PORTFOLIO SETUP: WRITING A DESCRIPTION

• On page 173 of the Student Edition, students are asked to write a formal report that describes. Students can think about a report they might have to write and use the steps outlined in this chapter to write it. If students have difficulty coming up with ideas for these reports, ask students to meet in small groups and brainstorm ideas for each student's report. Approve each student's report topic, making certain that the ideas are neither too broad nor too narrow.

CD-ROM TEAMWORK/COOPERATIVE ACTIVITY

• This exercise focuses on the difference between formal and informal writing. This is an important distinction for students to learn to make. First, students do research by talking to teachers and other adults. Then, students discuss what they have learned and complete a chart that helps them to distinguish between the two kinds of writing. Finally, the group writes a formal and informal report and compares the two.

LESSON PLANNING CHART			
CHAPTER 8	**STUDENT EDITION PAGES**	**TEACHER'S RESOURCE MANUAL PAGES**	**CD-ROM**
Writing/Reading Activities	149, 150, 153, 157, 160, 161, 164, 169–173	63–66, 68–73	✓
Speaking/Listening Activities	149, 156, 164, 172, 173	63, 66, 67, 69, 71	✓
Career Activities	149, 160	66	✓
Critical Thinking Activities	148, 149, 151, 154, 158, 160, 162, 164, 165, 172, 173	63, 64, 66, 69, 72	✓
Vocabulary Activities	147, 172	64	✓
ESL/LEP Tips		64, 67, 71, 72	
Teamwork/Cooperative Activities	149, 156, 164	63, 64, 67, 69, 71	✓
Curriculum Connections		67, 69	
Technology Activities	153, 171	72, 84	

Reading Reports
Student Edition, pages 148–149

INTO
Using Prior Knowledge
Ask students to describe how they read a report. Do they preview the headings and the graphics? Do they just begin reading it without previewing it? Ask students to preview the lesson headings and captions and predict what they will learn about reading reports.

THROUGH
Developing the Lesson
Students learn the differences between formal and informal reports. Informal reports include sales and incident reports, while formal reports include research reports. The lesson offers the Cornell Note-taking Strategy for reading research reports. Ask students to use this strategy as discussed on page 149 of the Student Edition. You might consider distributing the graphic organizer for the Cornell Note-taking Strategy that can be found on the CD-ROM.

Discussing Visuals Review Figures 8-1 and 8-2 on pages 148 and 149 of the Student Edition. How can students tell if they are reading a formal or informal report? What are the steps of reading research reports?

BEYOND
Closing the Lesson
Ask teams to exchange the incident reports they wrote for the *Apply What You Learn* activity. Ask students to use the Cornell Note-taking Strategy on page 149 of the Student Edition when reading the report. Is it complete? Does it address all the issues surrounding the incident? Is there enough detail to clearly describe the incident?

Extending the Lesson
Ask students to look at Figure 8-1 on page 148 of the Student Edition. Suppose the management of a hypothetical company wanted a formal sales report to send to the president of the company. How could students revise the sales report in Figure 8-1 so that it would be appropriate to send to the president?

ESL/LEP Tip
Students learning English may have difficulty understanding the difference between formal and informal reports. Ask English-proficient students to help students define the terms *formal* and *informal.* Then, ask English-proficient students to work with students to identify the qualities that distinguish formal writing from informal writing by looking at samples of each one. Is one report longer than the other? What is each report describing?

Grammar Workshop

TIP

Tell students to develop mnemonic devices that are easy for them to remember because these will help them differentiate between confusing word pairs.

Lesson Resources

On the *CD-ROM*

- Grammar Workshop Practice: Practicing Word Choice
- Grammar Workshop Test: Practicing Word Choice

In the *Handbook*

- Commonly Confused Words: 366–371

PRACTICING WORD CHOICE

Grammar Workshop at-a-Glance

Students learn the difference between confusing pairs of words, such as *accept* and *except*, *affect* and *effect*, *among* and *between*, *fewer* and *less*, and *good* and *well*.

Error Alert: Solving the Problem

- Ask students, *What does* accept *mean?* (to receive) *What does* except *mean?* (but, other than)

- Write this sentence on the chalkboard: *I (accept, except) this award on behalf of my project team.*

- Ask students, *Which one of these words is the correct word choice?* (accept) *How do you know?*

- *Is there any device that you could use to help yourself remember the difference?* (They could connect *except* with *exceptional*.)

- Write this sentence on the chalkboard: *Customers with (fewer, less) than 10 items may use the express check-out counter.*

- Ask students, *What does* fewer *mean?* (refers to a number of separate items that can be counted) *What does* less *mean?* (refers to bulk amounts) *Which one of these words is the correct word choice?* (fewer) *Is there any device that you could use to help yourself remember the difference?*

- Write this sentence on the chalkboard: *Robert is doing very (good, well).*

- Ask students, Good *and* well *both mean the same thing, but when should each of them be used?* (Use *good* after linking verbs, such as *is, taste*, and *feel*; use *well* as an adverb.) *Which one of these words is the correct word choice?* (well) *Is there any device that you could use to help yourself remember the difference?*

- Ask students to work together to formulate devices to help them differentiate between the pairs of words listed on page 150 of the Student Edition. Then, ask students to create a sentence for each word in each pair. Students should explain why they chose each word.

Additional Resource From Globe Fearon:

- *Globe Exercise Books*
  Spelling and Vocabulary: 22–23

Collecting and Evaluating Information

Student Edition, pages 151–153

Student Edition, pages 151–153

LEARNING OBJECTIVE

▶ Students will learn how to collect and evaluate information to write a report.

Lesson Resources

On the CD-ROM

- Topic at-a-Glance: Evaluating Sources
- Application: Evaluating Sources

Additional Resources From Globe Fearon:

- *Globe Exercise Books*
  Paragraphs: 12–15
- *Survival Guide for Computer Literacy*: 105–106
- *Success in Writing*
  Writing to Explain: 25, 70
- *Writer's Toolkit*
  Handbook: Writing Handbook: Elements of Nonfiction: Using Resources

INTO

Using Prior Knowledge

Collecting and evaluating information is an important first step in creating a report. Create a word web. In the middle circle, write *Sources of information*. Then, ask students to name sources they might use when writing a report. Connect each idea to *Sources of information*. Then, ask students to preview the lesson headings and captions and predict what they will learn about collecting and evaluating information.

THROUGH

Developing the Lesson

Students learn the differences between primary and secondary sources. Students also learn how to locate printed sources, such as books and magazines in a library, how to search the Internet, how to set up and get the most out of an interview, and how to evaluate each of their sources. Discuss the information under each heading with students. What kind of information would they look for on the Internet? When would they use an interview? Ask students to supply uses for each source. For example, tell students to imagine they are researching fitness clubs for a client who wants to open one. How could they use each of these sources to find information?

BEYOND

Closing the Lesson

Ask students to review the list of sources they have compiled for the *Apply What You Learn* activity. Ask students to explain why they chose each source. Was one of the sources the only one with certain information? Do any of the sources have informative graphics? Is the interviewee an expert on the subject? Then, ask students to evaluate each of their sources using the questions on page 153 of the Student Edition as a guide. Once students have answered each of the questions for each source, ask them to write a one-sentence analysis of the accuracy and validity of their sources.

Job Path Project

Interviewing is an important job-search skill. Ask students to locate and interview a professional in their chosen field. Suggest that students use the Checklist for Writing Interview Questions on page 153 of the Student Edition to draft a list of questions. Students can take notes on the interview, make an outline of the main points, and write an essay about what they have learned.

Choosing a Method of Organization

Student Edition, pages 154–156

LEARNING OBJECTIVE

▶ Students will learn ways to organize information to write a report.

Lesson Resources

 On the *CD-ROM*

• Topic at-a-Glance: Using Graphic Organizers to Organize Information

• Application: Using Graphic Organizers to Organize Information

• Various graphic organizers

 In the *Handbook*

• Strategies for Organizing Your Writing: 338–339

Additional Resources From Globe Fearon:

• *Globe Exercise Books*
Paragraphs: 16–21

• *Success in Writing*
Writing to Describe: 70
Writing to Explain: 10–11

• *Writer's Toolkit*
Organizing Details: Venn Diagram

• *Be a Better Reader*
Level G: 170

INTO

Using Prior Knowledge

There are many ways to organize information. It is important to select a method that fits the topic. Write these phrases on the chalkboard: *time order, comparison-and-contrast order,* and *order of importance.* Ask students to speculate about which topics may fit with each method of organization. Then, ask students to preview the lesson headings and captions and predict what they will learn about choosing a method of organization.

THROUGH

Developing the Lesson

Students will learn the parts of a report: *introduction, body,* and *conclusion.* Students will also learn that reports can be organized in the following ways: chronologically, using comparison-and-contrast order, by order of importance, or by combining these.

Discussing Visuals Review each of the methods of organization using Figures 8-3, 8-4, 8-5, and 8-6 on pages 154–156 of the Student Edition as examples. You may consider using the graphic organizers located on the CD-ROM to explain these methods. The timeline, for example, can be used to organize information in chronological order.

BEYOND

Closing the Lesson

After students complete the *Apply What You Learn* activity, divide the class into groups. Ask each group to brainstorm a topic that would work for each method of organization. Ask groups to exchange papers with each other and match the topic with the method of organization. Then, ask students to recommend a second method for organizing the material.

ESL/LEP Tip

Ask English-proficient students to work with students to review the purpose of each graphic organizer and the organizational method it represents. Ask English-proficient students to help students understand how each of the organizational methods works.

Curriculum Connection: Science

Ask students to bring their science textbooks to class. Have them work in groups to identify two different organizational methods in the book. Then, ask students to explain why they think the author of the book chose a particular method to organize the material.

Grammar Workshop

TIP

Tell students that they can correct errors with parallelism by making sure that similar forms in a sentence use the same tense or structure.

Lesson Resources

 **On the CD-ROM**

- Grammar Workshop Practice: Using Parallel Construction
- Grammar Workshop Test: Using Parallel Construction

In the Handbook

- Parallel Construction: 341

USING PARALLEL CONSTRUCTION

Grammar Workshop at-a-Glance

This Grammar Workshop addresses parallelism in nouns, verbs, phrases, and clauses. It explains how to use parallel construction correctly.

Error Alert: Solving the Problem

- Write this sentence on the chalkboard: *The computer technician ordered new monitors, computer, and cables for the entire staff.*

- Ask students, *What part of this sentence doesn't sound correct?* (computer) *How can we make this sentence parallel in construction?* (change *computer* to *computers*)

- Write this sentence on the chalkboard: *Our company finds answers, providing solutions, and directs workflow.*

- Ask students, *Which grammatical form in this sentence is not parallel in construction?* (verb) *How can we make the sentence on the chalkboard parallel in construction?* (change *providing* to *provides*)

- Write this sentence on the chalkboard: *Logan is good at organizing information, evaluating sources, and outlines his research.*

- Ask students, *Which grammatical form in this sentence is not parallel in construction?* (phrase) *How can we make the sentence on the chalkboard parallel in construction?* (change *outlines* to *outlining*)

Write these sentences on the chalkboard. Ask students to identify the grammatical form that is not parallel in construction. Then, ask students to make the sentence parallel in construction. Answers are in parentheses.

1. The choices at the picnic were swimming, playing games, and to eat as much food as you wanted. (eating)

2. The job requires a keen eye, a steady hand, and working with delicate machinery. (an ability to work)

3. Brad was looking for a job that would allow him to learn about computers, run the office equipment, and to interact with customers. (to run)

4. In the newspaper's early days, everyone sold advertisements, distributed newspapers, and writing stories. (wrote stories)

Additional Resources From Globe Fearon:

- *Globe Exercise Books*
  Sentences: 18–19

- *Success in Writing*:
  Grammar Skills for Writers: 24–25

Creating an Outline
Student Edition, pages 158–160

LEARNING OBJECTIVE

▶ Students will learn how to create an outline before writing.

Lesson Resources

 On the CD-ROM

- Topic at-a-Glance: Creating an Outline
- Application: Creating an Outline
- Graphic Organizer: Using the Outlining Strategy

Additional Resources
From Globe Fearon:

- *Globe Exercise Books*
  Paragraphs: 8–9

- *Success in Writing*
  Writing to Explain: 72

- *Reading in the Content Areas*
  Level A: 8–11
  Level C: 8–11

- *Be a Better Reader*
  Level B: 140–141
  Level C: 92–93
  Level D: 116–117
  Level E: 92–93
  Level F: 112–113

- *Writer's Toolkit*
  Organizing Details: Outliner

INTO

Using Prior Knowledge

Ask students how an outline can be used as an organizational tool. Why is an outline useful to a writer? Discuss how outlining can help students decide on the structure of a paper *before* they begin writing. Ask students to preview the lesson headings and captions and predict what they will learn about creating an outline.

THROUGH

Developing the Lesson

Students will learn the steps involved in writing an outline. Students are introduced to two kinds of outlines: a topic outline and a sentence outline. Once students have written an outline, they will learn how to review it before they begin writing their report.

Discussing Visuals Review Figure 8-7, *Writing in the Real World: Outline*, on page 159 of the Student Edition. Discuss each of the callouts, and help students identify the main idea, the topic headings, and the subtopics.

BEYOND

Closing the Lesson

Ask students to review the outline they wrote for the *Apply What You Learn* activity by using the checklist on page 160 of the Student Edition. After students review their outlines, ask them to exchange them with one another. Then, ask students to put themselves in the place of the shop owner and review a classmate's outline. Based on the information in the outline, would students say that this neighborhood would be the best place to open a store? Why or why not?

Extending the Lesson

Ask students to rewrite their outlines from the *Apply What You Learn* activity. If they used a topic outline, ask them to write a sentence outline. If they used a sentence outline, ask them to use a topic outline. Then, ask students to exchange papers with a classmate. Ask students to review their classmate's outlines using the checklist on page 160 of the Student Edition.

Curriculum Connection: Social Studies

Ask students to outline a chapter from their social studies books. Will they use a topic outline or a sentence outline? How does this help organize information that they are trying to learn?

Grammar Workshop

TIP

Remind students that collective nouns can take singular or plural verbs or pronouns. If the collective noun names a group of people, things, or animals that act as a unit, it takes a singular verb or pronoun. If the collective noun refers to each person as an individual, it takes a plural verb or pronoun.

Lesson Resources

On the CD-ROM

• Grammar Workshop Practice: Making Collective Nouns Agree with Their Verbs and Pronouns

• Grammar Workshop Test: Making Collective Nouns Agree with Their Verbs and Pronouns

• Handbook Practice: Subject–Verb Agreement

In the Handbook

• Subject–Verb Agreement: 347–348

Additional Resource From Globe Fearon:

• *Globe Exercise Books* *Mechanics and Usage*: 8–9

MAKING COLLECTIVE NOUNS AGREE WITH THEIR VERBS AND PRONOUNS

Grammar Workshop at-a-Glance

In this Grammar Workshop, students learn to identify collective nouns. They also learn how to make sure the verbs and pronouns they use agree with the collective nouns.

Error Alert: Solving the Problem

• Write this sentence on the chalkboard: *The jury (is, are) ready to make its decision.*

• Ask students, *Which is the correct verb?* (is) *Why?* (The collective noun takes a singular pronoun when it refers to a group as a unit.)

• Write this sentence on the chalkboard: *After the verdict, the jury (was, were) ready to leave for their homes across the city.*

• Ask students, *Which is the correct verb?* (was) *Why?* (A jury is made up of several individuals, but it is acting as one unit.)

• Write this sentence on the chalkboard: *A group of employees (is, are) expected to work on four different projects.*

• Ask students, *Which is the correct verb?* (are) *Why?* (because *group* refers to *employees*)

Write these sentences on the chalkboard. Ask students to identify the collective noun and whether it takes a singular verb or a plural verb. Then, ask students to rewrite each sentence to include a pronoun that agrees with the collective noun.

1. The jury (disagrees, disagree) on a verdict. (disagrees)

2. The jury (has, have) reached a verdict. (has)

3. Our committee (is, are) making the report. (is)

4. Some on the committee (is, are) pointing fingers at management. (are)

5. Last year's class (is, are) planning a reunion. (is)

6. Last year's class now (live, lives) in several states. (live)

7. The crowd (demands, demand) an accounting. (demands)

8. The crowd (know, knows) themselves well. (know)

9. The team (plans, plan) to win. (plans)

10. The team (walks, walk) home after practice. (walk)

Using Relevant Details

Student Edition, pages 162–164

LEARNING OBJECTIVE

▶ Students will learn how to use relevant, supporting details in a research report.

Lesson Resources

On the *CD-ROM*

• Topic at-a-Glance: Using Relevant Details

• Application: Using Relevant Details

INTO

Using Prior Knowledge

Ask students to brainstorm why details are important. How do details help students communicate their ideas? Ask students to think about an island. Then, ask them how their picture changes when they pair it with the following adjectives: *tropical*, *secluded*, *arctic*, and *over-populated*. How do these adjectives help create a picture? Is it different from the one the students originally thought of? Ask students to preview the lesson headings and captions and predict what they will learn about using relevant details.

THROUGH

Developing the Lesson

Students learn why and how to use details. They also learn how to choose relevant details, and they learn about different kinds of details, such as facts, statistics, quotations, definitions, anecdotes, examples, reasons, and comparisons.

Discussing Visuals Review Figure 8–9 on page 163 of the Student Edition with students. Discuss the different types of details, asking students to suggest an example of each one. What kinds of reports might use statistics? a quotation? a comparison? Why? What is the benefit of using a detail such as an anecdote?

BEYOND

Closing the Lesson

Ask students to refer to the *Apply What You Learn* activity on page 164. Have students work in pairs and choose Figure 8–10 or Figure 8–11 on page 164 of the Student Edition. Then, ask students to remove all the details that appear in the figure they have chosen. How does this alter the meaning of the selection? Finally, ask students to rewrite the paragraph using new details.

ESL/LEP Tip

Ask English-proficient students to work with students to explain the different kinds of details. Ask students to use their textbooks to work together and find examples of each kind of detail. Then, ask English-proficient students to identify the kind of detail each one represents.

Extending the Lesson

Ask students to describe a favorite book or movie. Suggest that students use relevant details that appeal to the senses. For example, rather than saying, "It was the funniest movie I ever saw," students should give details of what made it funny.

Additional Resource From Globe Fearon:

• *Globe Exercise Books*
  Paragraphs: 14–15

Writing the Formal Report
Student Edition, pages 165–169

LEARNING OBJECTIVE

▶ Students will learn how to write a formal report.

Lesson Resources

On the *CD-ROM*

• Topic at-a-Glance: Writing the Formal Report

• Application: Checklist for Writing the Formal Report

• Application: Writing the Formal Report

Additional Resources
From Globe Fearon:

• *Globe Exercise Books*
 Paragraphs: 24–25, 32–33

• *Success in Writing*
 Writing to Explain: 28–37

• *Writer's Toolkit*
 Handbook: Writing Handbook: The Writing Process: Drafting; Revising and Editing: Unity and Coherence Checker: Elements of Nonfiction: Bibliography, Citing Sources

INTO

Using Prior Knowledge

When students write their drafts, they will see the value of the time they spent collecting and evaluating information, choosing a method of organization, creating an outline, and choosing relevant details. Ask students to discuss reports they have written. What were the topics? How did they research them? How did they organize their information? Ask students to preview the lesson headings and captions and predict what they will learn about writing the formal report.

THROUGH

Developing the Lesson

Students learn how to draft a report, why and how to use formal language, how to write footnotes and endnotes, how to compile a bibliography, and how to edit and publish a report. Discuss the sample footnotes and endnotes on page 166 of the Student Edition. What kinds of information do these citations contain?

Discussing Visuals Review Figure 8-12, *Writing in the Real World: Formal Report, Part 1*, and Figure 8–13, *Writing in the Real World: Formal Report, Part 2*, on pages 167 and 168 of the Student Edition. Discuss the callouts. What is the purpose of each part of a formal report?

BEYOND

Closing the Lesson

Ask students to refer to the example footnotes and endnotes from the *Apply What You Learn* activity on page 169 of the Student Edition. Ask students to think about the kinds of information each of these citations contains. Why is it important for students to provide this information for their readers? Ask students to write a brief explanation of their answers.

ESL/LEP Tip

The form of footnotes and bibliography seems mystifying to many students, but, to those learning English, the additional rules governing footnotes and bibliography can be even harder to understand. Review the footnotes and bibliographic entries on page 166 of the Student Edition. Point out each punctuation mark so that students understand the format for these citations.

Web Activity

Ask students to think about how formal reports on the Internet differ from reports printed on paper. Ask students to search the Internet for an example of a formal report. Do formal reports on the Internet include a title page? a table of contents? a bibliography?

Grammar Workshop

Student Edition, page 170

AVOIDING REDUNDANCIES

Grammar Workshop at-a-Glance

This Grammar Workshop shows students how to avoid redundancies when they write. It also includes examples of redundant phrases.

Error Alert: Solving the Problem

- Write this sentence on the chalkboard: *Once we had written down the instructions, we saw that the same, identical steps could be used.*

- Ask students, *What word can be eliminated without changing the meaning of the sentence?* (identical)

- Ask students, *Why can* identical *be eliminated?* (because it has the same meaning as *same*)

- Ask students, *Why is it important to eliminate redundancies?* (They can distract and confuse readers.)

Write these examples on the chalkboard. Ask students to identify the redundant clusters of words. Then, ask them to rewrite the sentences to eliminate the redundancies.

1. We were late because he circled around the block five times. (We were late because he circled the block five times.)

2. The same exact problems showed up in the plan of action. (The same problems showed up in the plan of action.)

3. We have no future plans. (We have no plans.)

4. It is a known fact that he makes all his furniture by hand. (It is a fact that he makes all his furniture by hand.)

5. I myself am not willing to deny the known facts. (I am not willing to deny the facts.)

6. I would like to have a verbal discussion with the employees about overtime. (I would like to have a discussion with the employees about overtime.)

7. This report represents the sum total of our hard work. (This report represents the total of our hard work.)

8. She said that she might possibly make the meeting. (She said that she might make the meeting.)

TIP

Although it is very important to include details when writing, it is necessary to avoid redundancies. Explain to students that details enhance a report, but redundancy can make reading tedious.

Lesson Resources

On the *CD-ROM*

- Grammar Workshop Practice: Avoiding Redundancies
- Grammar Workshop Test: Avoiding Redundancies

In the *Handbook*

- Redundancies: 342

CHAPTER 8 • WRITING REPORTS THAT DESCRIBE **73**

Student Edition, pages 174–175

WRITING TO PERSUADE
English in Context

TEACHING THE CHAPTER OPENER

Carla works as a pet groomer in a small shop, and she performs many of the services it offers. Her boss wants her to take on the new responsibility of writing a newspaper advertisement and sales letter to attract more business. Chapter 9 will give students experience with business-related, persuasive writing.

• Ask students to think of jobs they might have five years from now. List them on the chalkboard. Then, have students suggest types of persuasive writing they might be asked to do in each of these jobs.

PORTFOLIO SETUP: WRITING A PERSUASIVE AD AND SALES LETTER ✉

• On page 199 of the Student Edition, students are asked to write an ad and a sales letter. As you begin this chapter, discuss the Portfolio Project. Ask students to think about products or services they might like to sell. Then, ask them to maintain a running list of ideas for their ads and their sales letters as they work through the chapter. What kinds of graphics could they include? Does their company have a logo? What kind of ad would attract their attention? You might want to bring in and show sample ads to give students ideas of what their work might look like.

CD-ROM TEAMWORK/COOPERATIVE ACTIVITY 👥

• This exercise asks students to think of a school event that should be publicized and to form groups to work on publicity for the event. Each student in the group can choose to take on the role of researcher, writer, editor, or publicist. This worksheet will help students keep track of who is responsible for each task, as well as the group's progress.

LESSON PLANNING CHART			
CHAPTER 9	**STUDENT EDITION PAGES**	**TEACHER'S RESOURCE MANUAL PAGES**	**CD-ROM**
Writing/Reading Activities	177, 180, 181, 183, 187, 188, 191, 192, 196–200	74–83	✓
Speaking/Listening Activities	177, 183, 187, 191, 196, 197	74–76, 79, 81, 83	✓
Career Activities	199, 200	78, 81	✓
Critical Thinking Activities	176–178, 182–184, 187, 189, 193, 198, 199	74–76, 78, 81, 83	✓
Vocabulary Activities	175, 198		✓
ESL/LEP Tips		79	
Teamwork/Cooperative Activities	183, 187, 191, 197	74, 75, 79, 81, 83	✓
Curriculum Connections		76, 78	
Technology Activities	197	83, 84	

Reading Persuasive Writing

Student Edition, pages 176–177

LEARNING OBJECTIVE

▶ Students will learn to recognize and read persuasive writing.

Lesson Resources

In the *Handbook*

- Reading Strategies: 332–336
- Modes of Writing: 344

Additional Resources From Globe Fearon:

- *Globe Exercise Books*
  Paragraphs: 36–37

- *Be a Better Reader*
  Level B: 170
  Level D: 172–173
  Level G: 95

- *Writer's Toolkit*
  Inspirations for Writing:
  Modes: Persuasion;
  Writing Handbook: Elements of Nonfiction: Propaganda Techniques

INTO

Using Prior Knowledge

The goal of persuasive writing is to convince a reader of something. Persuasive writing can appear in several places, including catalogs and advertisements. Ask students to brainstorm the kinds of persuasive writing found in catalogs and advertisements. How many of the examples might be written for or by a businessperson? Discuss how persuasive writing is used in business. Then, ask students to preview the lesson headings and captions and predict what they will learn about reading persuasive writing.

THROUGH

Developing the Lesson

Students will learn to identify types of persuasive writing, such as that found in catalogs, advertisements, press releases, and on billboards. Students also learn a strategy for reading persuasive writing.

Discussing Visuals Discuss with students Figure 9-1 on page 176 of the Student Edition. How can they tell if this is a press release? Why do they think the company wrote this press release? Is this an example of persuasive writing? Why or why not?

BEYOND

Closing the Lesson

Ask students to review the examples of persuasive writing they analyzed in the *Apply What You Learn* activity. Ask them to choose the piece of persuasive writing they find least persuasive and rewrite it so that it is more effective. What did they change? Why? Ask students to exchange their original ads and revisions with a classmate. Which one do they find more persuasive? Why? You may wish to create a bulletin board that displays all of the persuasive writing samples that students collected for this assignment.

Extending the Lesson

Persuasive writing can be found in junk mail. Ask students to ask their parents if they can sort through unwanted junk mail to find examples of effective and ineffective persuasive writing. Ask volunteers to present a piece of junk mail and explain why it contains writing that is either persuasive or not persuasive.

Techniques of Persuasive Writing

Student Edition, pages 178–180

LEARNING OBJECTIVE

▶ Students will learn the techniques of persuasive writing.

Lesson Resources

On the *CD-ROM*

• Topic at-a-Glance: Techniques of Persuasive Writing

• Topic at-a-Glance: Persuasive Writing Model

• Application: Techniques of Persuasive Writing

INTO

Using Prior Knowledge

Persuasive writing uses particular techniques to convince an audience. Ask students to think about examples of persuasive writing. What kinds of techniques do these examples use to appeal to a reader? Why do students think these techniques are effective? Record students' answers on the chalkboard. Then, ask students to preview the lesson headings and captions and predict what they will learn about techniques of persusasive writing.

THROUGH

Developing the Lesson

Students will learn how to consider purpose and audience when writing persuasively. They will learn how tone, self-interest, emotion, and evidence are used to make writing persuasive. Students will also learn that persuasive writing often ends with a call to action that appeals directly to a reader. Finally, students will learn about evidence that can be used to support persuasive writing.

Discussing Visuals Review with students Figures 9-2, 9-3, 9-4, and 9-5 on pages 178 and 179 of the Student Edition. For whom were each of these examples written? What makes each of them effective? ineffective? Review Figure 9-6 on page 180 of the Student Edition with students. Ask students to brainstorm additional examples for each kind of evidence.

BEYOND

Closing the Lesson

Ask students to refer to one of the samples they used for the *Apply What You Learn* activity. Ask students to review Figure 9-6 on page 180 of the Student Edition. Then, ask students to choose a sample that uses evidence. What kinds of evidence do their samples use? Is it effective? ineffective? Why?

Extending the Lesson

Using the examples of persuasive business writing that students have been collecting, ask them to identify three examples of persuasive writing techniques. Why did the writer use these techniques?

Curriculum Connection: Social Studies

Ask students to read the "Letters to the Editor" column in their school or community newspaper. Then, ask students to identify the purpose and audience, persuasive writing techniques, call to action, and evidence in one of the letters.

Additional Resources
From Globe Fearon:

• *Globe Exercise Books*
  Paragraphs: 10–11

• *Success in Writing*
  Writing to Persuade: 23–25

• *Writer's Toolkit*
  Considering Audience and Purpose

TIP

When using a conjunction such as *and, or, but yet, so*, or *nor*, remind students to insert a comma before the conjunction to separate the two independent clauses.

Lesson Resources

On the *CD-ROM*

- Grammar Workshop Practice: Using Conjunctions
- Grammar Workshop Test: Using Conjunctions
- Handbook Practice: Conjunctions

In the *Handbook*

- Conjunctions: 355–356

Additional Resources From Globe Fearon:

- *Globe Exercise Books*
  Parts of Speech: 40–43

- *Success in Writing*
  Grammar Skills for Writers: 40–41

- *Writer's Toolkit*
  Handbook: Grammar
  Handbook: Prepositions, Conjunctions, and Interjections

USING CONJUNCTIONS

Grammar Workshop at-a-Glance

This Grammar Workshop focuses on conjunctions. It explains coordinating conjunctions, which connect words, phrases, and clauses with the same grammatical structure; correlative conjunctions, which are conjunctions that are used in pairs; and subordinating conjunctions, which join dependent clauses to independent clauses.

Error Alert: Solving the Problem

- Write this sentence on the chalkboard: *Sharon found the receipts Janice made the adjustments.*

- Ask students, *What are the two separate thoughts in this sentence?* (Sharon found the receipts. Janice made the adjustments.)

- Ask students, *How can we join these two separate thoughts?* (Sharon found the receipts, and Janice made the adjustments.)

- Ask students, *How does the word change how the sentence reads?* (It shows how the two are connected.)

- Write this sentence on the chalkboard: *Either he was on time nor he wasn't.*

- Ask students, *Is this sentence correct?* (no; *nor* should be *or*)

- Write this sentence on the chalkboard: *Johnny will miss lunch unless he arrives soon.*

- Ask students, *What is the independent clause in this sentence?* (Johnny will miss lunch)

- Ask students, *What is the dependent clause in this sentence?* (unless he arrives soon)

- Ask students, *What does the word* unless *do?* (It shows how the clauses are related)

🖉 Write the following sentences on the chalkboard. Ask students to underline and identify the type of conjunction in each sentence.

1. The new phone system is expensive, <u>but</u> it is easy to use.

2. <u>Unless</u> you have a different solution, we will try this one.

3. The teams <u>neither</u> attended the meeting <u>nor</u> were invited.

4. Please let me know <u>before</u> I get started.

5. Marc and Kurt are coworkers, <u>but</u> they are also good friends.

Using Graphics to Persuade

Student Edition, pages 182–183

LEARNING OBJECTIVE

▶ Students will learn how to use graphics to persuade.

Lesson Resources

On the CD-ROM

• Topics at-a-Glance: Using Graphics to Persuade

• Application: Using Graphics to Persuade

INTO

Using Prior Knowledge

Graphics present information in a visual way. Ask students to listen carefully to this data: Harcount Candy sold 30 units in its first year, 90 in its second, and 120 in its third, while New Hampshire Candy sold 40 units in its first year, 60 in its second, and 90 in its third. Which company sold more candy in its second year? Now, draw a line graph on the chalkboard to illustrate this information, and ask the same question in order to demonstrate how effective a graph can be to portray information. Tell students to preview the lesson headings and captions and predict what they will learn about using graphics to persuade.

THROUGH

Developing the Lesson

Students learn the differences between graphs, charts, and tables. The lesson then discusses bar graphs, pictographs, and data tables.

Discussing Visuals Review Figures 9-7, 9-8, and 9-9 on pages 182 and 183 of the Student Edition. What might each of these graphics be trying to persuade the reader to think or do?

BEYOND

Closing the Lesson

Ask students to use the data table from the *Apply What You Learn* activity and assess its visual persuasiveness. Would they be persuaded by the information in the table? What would make this data table more persuasive?

Curriculum Connection: Math

Another type of graphic that is often used is a circle graph, which shows how a whole item or amount is divided. Ask students to research how to create a circle graph. Then, ask them to complete one. Possible topics include how a student spends his or her money, what activities occupy a day, and what the different costs are within a company's budget.

Job Path Project

Ask students to review their Career reports and find statistics about their fields that could be represented in one of the types of graphics shown. For example, students can graph an industry's profits over a four-year period. If students are unable to find statistics, ask them to create a graphic that shows the number of people employed in that field in 1980, 1990, and 2000.

Writing a Sales Letter

Student Edition, pages 184–187

LEARNING OBJECTIVE

▶ Students will learn how to write a sales letter.

Lesson Resource

On the CD-ROM

• Topic at-a-Glance: Writing a Sales Letter

INTO

Using Prior Knowledge

The purpose of a sales letter is to persuade a reader to buy something. Bring to class a sales letter that you received. Read it aloud to the students. Ask students to guess what you just read and tell them it was a sales letter. Ask students to preview the lesson headings and captions and predict what they will learn about writing a sales letter.

THROUGH

Developing the Lesson

Students learn about the types of sales letters, which include personal appeals, direct mailings, and mass mailings, and what to look for in these kinds of sales letters. Students learn how to create a sales letter by researching the product or service, thinking about customers' needs, getting the readers' attention, stating the purpose, presenting the evidence, and concluding with a strong argument and a call to action.

Discussing Visuals Review Figure 9-10, *Writing in the Real World: Sales Letter*, on page 186 of the Student Edition. Ask students to identify each of the steps used to create the sales letter in Figure 9-10. How does the letter in Figure 9-10 consider customer needs? get the readers' attention? Does it conclude with a strong argument and a call to action?

BEYOND

Closing the Lesson

Divide the class into groups, and ask each group to choose the least persuasive sales letter from the *Apply What You Learn* activity. Then, ask each group to rewrite its sales letter to make the letter more effective. What would make each letter more persuasive? Ask each group to read its letter to the class.

ESL/LEP Tip

Show students learning English how tone can vary in this kind of writing. Find examples of different tones, such as aggressive or friendly tones, in various sales letters. Help students determine how different words and punctuation can change the way a letter reads.

Extending the Lesson

Ask students to begin working on the Portfolio Project on page 199 of the Student Edition. Ask students to follow the steps for creating a sales letter for the product or service they chose at the beginning of the chapter and for which they will be writing a press release later.

Additional Resource
From Globe Fearon:

• *Success in Writing*
Writing to Persuade: 68–69

Grammar Workshop

TIP

Mnemonic devices can help students remember the distinction between some commonly confused words, such as *its* and *it's*; *than* and *then*; *there*, *their*, and *they're*; and *to*, *too*, and *two*. For example, *than* is a conjunction that connects two parts of a comparison. *Then* usually refers to time. Both *then* and *time* have the letter *e*.

Lesson Resources

On the *CD-ROM*

• Grammar Workshop Practice: Using Homophones Correctly
• Grammar Workshop Test: Using Homophones Correctly

In the *Handbook*

• Commonly Confused Words: 366–371

Additional Resources From Globe Fearon:

• *Globe Exercise Books*
  Spelling and Vocabulary: 22–23

• *Success in Writing*
  Grammar Skills for Writers: 108–109

USING HOMOPHONES CORRECTLY

Grammar Workshop at-a-Glance

This Grammar Workshop helps students use homophones correctly. This Grammar Workshop addresses *its* and *it's*; *than* and *then*; *there*, *their*, and *they're*; and *to*, *too*, and *two*.

Error Alert: Solving the Problem

• Write this sentence on the chalkboard: *The team has (its, it's) own assistant.*

• Ask students, *Does anyone know which word is correct?* (its)

• Ask students, *Can you think of a mnemonic device for* its *and* it's? (Read *it's* as *it is*. If the sentence makes sense, that is the correct choice.)

• Write this sentence on the chalkboard: *(There, Their, They're) going to leave (there, their, they're) car over (there, their, they're).*

• Tell students, *You can use the same trick with* they're, *as above. Read* they're *as* they are. *To tell the difference between* there *and* their, *remember that* there *refers to a place and both* there *and* place *end in* e. *All others are* their.

• Ask students, *Using our new device, what is the correct answer?* (They're going to leave their car over there.)

• Write this sentence on the chalkboard: *Those (to, too, two) reports are (to, too, two) long (to, too, two) fit in one binder.*

• Tell students, *Most of us know* two *as the number 2, but how can we tell the other two words apart? Remember that* too *can mean* more, *and there are more o's in* too *than there are in* to. *All others are* to.

• Ask students, *Using our new device, what is the correct answer?* (Those two reports are too long to fit in one binder.)

• Ask students, *Can you think of a device for "than" and "then"?*

Write these sentences on the chalkboard. Ask students to rewrite each sentence, choosing the correct word in parentheses.

1. Are we meeting them (there, their, and they're)? (there)

2. I'd like to go, (to, too, two). (too)

3. (Its, It's) scheduled for later today. (It's)

4. Phoebe has a longer commute (than, then) Haley. (than)

Writing Ad and Catalog Copy
Student Edition, pages 189–191

INTO

Using Prior Knowledge

Like sales letters, advertisements and catalog copy are written to persuade a reader to buy something. Bring to class a variety of ads and catalogs. Post them and ask students what makes an ad or catalog an effective sales tool. Ask students to preview the lesson headings and captions and predict what they will learn about writing ad and catalog copy.

THROUGH

Developing the Lesson

Students learn about the parts of an advertisement, which include headlines, graphics, and copy. Students also learn how to write ad and catalog copy.

Discussing Visuals Review the basic features of the ad in Figure 9-11 on page 189 of the Student Edition. Then, ask students to analyze Figure 9-11. What makes this an effective or ineffective advertisement? Does it address the basic features of writing an advertisement? Review Figure 9-13 on page 191. What makes this an effective or ineffective advertisement? Would the students purchase this product on the basis of the catalog copy? You can use the ads you collected to help teach this lesson.

BEYOND

Closing the Lesson

Divide class into groups, and ask each group to refer to the ad and catalog copy they created for the *Apply What You Learn* activity. What audience did they write for? Ask students to choose a different audience and then rewrite the ad and the catalog copy for that audience. How is the second version different from the first? How did the tone change? How did the overall message change?

Job Path Project

Ask students to think about a product or service that might be advertised in their careers of choice. For example, if students chose restaurant manager, the restaurant may advertise a new dish or an entirely new menu of dinner selections. Ask students to create an ad for this product or service. Tell students to consider the audience, the tone, and the design of the ad. Ask students to place the finished work in their Career folders.

Grammar Workshop

TIP

There are three basic verb tenses: *past, present,* and *future.* Each of these can be used effectively to persuade a reader. For example: "You worked hard all year. Now is the time to reward yourself. By tomorrow, you will own a brand new car!"

Lesson Resources

On the *CD-ROM*

- Grammar Workshop Practice: Recognizing Verb Tenses
- Grammar Workshop Test: Recognizing Verb Tenses

In the *Handbook*

- Verb Tenses: 352–353

Additional Resources From Globe Fearon:

- *Globe Exercise Books*
Mechanics and Usage: 16–17
Parts of Speech: 12–13
Sentences: 24–25

- *Success in Writing*
Grammar Skills for Writers: 45, 50–51

- *Writer's Toolkit*
Handbook: Problem Solver: Incorrect Verb Tenses and Shifts

RECOGNIZING VERB TENSES

Grammar Workshop at-a-Glance

This Grammar Workshop teaches students how to recognize the verb tenses *past, present,* and *future.*

Error Alert: Solving the Problem

- Write this sentence on the chalkboard: *Jane wanted to buy a stereo.*

- Ask students, *Did Jane want to buy a stereo in the past, present, or future?* (past)

- Ask students, *How would you rewrite this sentence if Jane wanted to buy her stereo right now?* (Jane wants to buy a stereo.)

- Ask students, *How would you rewrite this sentence if Jane will want to buy her stereo in a month?* (Jane will want to buy a stereo.)

- Write this sentence on the chalkboard: *Cory talks frequently with his vendors.*

- Ask students, *Does Cory talk with his vendors in the past, present, or future?* (present)

- Ask students, *How would you rewrite this sentence if Cory already talked with his vendors?* (Cory talked frequently with his vendors.)

- Ask students, *How would you rewrite this sentence if Cory will talk to his vendors next week?* (Cory will talk frequently with his vendors.)

🖉 Write the following sentences on the chalkboard. Ask students to rewrite these sentences using the tense indicated.

1. We (future—to join) the group. (will join)

2. They (past—to attend) all the meetings. (attended)

3. You (present—to bring) the files. (bring *or* are bringing)

4. The assistant (past—to know) information technology. (knew)

5. We (present—to provide) a good-quality paper. (provide *or* are providing)

6. They (future—to distribute) the business directory. (will distribute)

7. I (present—to eat) lunch at that restaurant. (eat *or* am eating)

8. The committee (past—to plan) the meeting. (planned)

Writing a Press Release

Student Edition, pages 193–196

INTO

Using Prior Knowledge

Press releases announce newsworthy events. Create a press release. Pretend to be a news director at a television station, and ask students to imagine that they are the assistant directors. Review the press release with your students. Discuss what the press release contains and whether a reporter should do a story about the event. Ask students to preview the lesson headings and captions and predict what they will learn about writing a press release.

THROUGH

Developing the Lesson

Students learn what a press release is and when and how to write one. They use the five Ws—*who, what, when, where, why*—and *how*. Students learn how to gather and organize information, how to use a reporter's style, how to use quotations for interest, and how to watch for accuracy. Finally, students learn how to publish a press release by sending it to a news outlet.

Discussing Visuals Review Figure 9-14, *Writing in the Real World: Press Release*, on page 194 of the Student Edition. What is the purpose of this press release? How does it answer the five Ws? If you were the news director at a television station, would you assign a reporter to this story? Why?

BEYOND

Closing the Lesson

Ask students to exchange the press releases that they wrote for the *Apply What You Learn* activity with each other. Does the press release address the five Ws? Does it use a reporter's style? Were quotations used? Is it accurate?

Extending the Lesson

Students can continue work on the Portfolio Project on page 199 of the Student Edition. Ask them to write a press release to go along with the sales letter and ad they wrote for the product or service they chose. Ask students to exchange them with each other. Does the press release address the five Ws? Does it use a reporter's style? Were quotations used?

Web Activity

There are many additional tutorials on the Web for students who want to know more about writing press releases. Here are several:
www.xpresspress.com/PRnotes.html
www.newsbureau.com/tips/
www.pressflash.com/anatomy.html

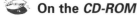

LEARNING OBJECTIVE

▶ Students will learn how to write a press release.

Lesson Resource

On the CD-ROM

• Topic at-a-Glance: Writing a Press Release

Formatting a Report
(Student Edition, page 171)

Formatting a report has become a required skill for many jobs. Make sure students know how to format a report by asking them to read the Tech Connection and type examples of the formatting discussed, such as font style and size. Ask students to explore the Page Setup of their word processing program and write a one-page report that explains what they learned. The report should show examples of each feature they explored.

Editing a Word-Processing Document
(Student Edition, page 197)

Most computer word-processing programs include tutorials on editing. Ask students to check the Help window to see if such a tutorial exists on their computers. If not, you might consider telling students to try these Web sites:

www.indiana.edu/~uitspubs/b045/
www.pcwebopedia.com/TERM/w/word_processing.html

Additional Resource
From Globe Fearon:

*Survival Guide for
Computer Literacy:* 60

WRITING IN BUSINESS

Student Edition, page 201

CAREER FILE PROJECT SUPPORT
On page 282 of the Student Edition, students will read about assistant store managers and bookkeeping or accounting clerks. Assistant store managers support their managers and interact with both the public and the store's employees. Bookkeeping or accounting clerks work with numbers, which makes attention to detail a critical part of their job. Ask students to think about the kinds of people who would be suitable for either of these jobs. How are they similar? How do they differ?

Action Profile
Ask students to choose one of the two careers profiled in this unit and answer the following questions:

1. What experience, education, and training do employers expect of those they hire?
2. Are there any local or state requirements for working in this field?
3. What interests and traits do you have that would make this a good job for you?
4. Does the job have any requirements you might have difficulty meeting?
5. What related fields might interest you?

Business writing has special requirements. Employees who want to succeed in business need to feel comfortable writing business letters, proposals, and technical materials. The ability to write coherent business letters, to put ideas into proposals, or to write clear and detailed manuals make employees valuable assets to a company.

What's in the Unit

This unit begins with Chapter 10, which is about writing business letters. Students learn the correct form to use, the reasons for writing business letters, and how to write letters that will be read and answered. Chapter 11 addresses writing proposals, which are written plans of action designed to improve a situation, solve a problem, or persuade a customer to use a company's product. In Chapter 12, students learn to read and write technical reports. They learn that this type of writing explains how a product or process works and that it conveys complex ideas so nonexperts can understand them.

Previewing the Unit

Write the words *business letters, proposals,* and *technical writing* on the chalkboard. Ask students for definitions of these terms. Write students' answers on the chalkboard. Ask students to preview the unit by looking at the titles, headings, subheadings, figures, photos, illustrations, captions, and key words. Then, discuss why students' ability to write these kinds of materials might make a difference in their careers.

Developing the Unit

Students probably understand the importance of writing business letters, but they may not know why writing proposals and technical reports is important. Reinforce the importance of these business skills by asking students to research how proposals and technical writing play a part in the careers they are investigating. Ask students to interview people who work in their careers of choice and find examples of how these kinds of writing are used.

BLOCK SCHEDULING TIP
90-Minute Session Organizer for Lessons 10-1 and 10-2

ACTIVITY	MINUTES
Preview lesson headings, captions, and boldfaced words; brainstorm uses of business writing and show examples of business letters	10
Read and discuss Lessons 10-1 and 10-2	20
Small groups meet to discuss *Apply What You Learn*, Lesson 10-1	10
Writing: Ask students to write a marketing plan.	20
Discuss Grammar Workshop: Using Irregular Verbs	15
Small group meets to discuss *Apply What You Learn*, Lesson 10-2	10
Concluding reflections, assignments, and answer questions	5

IN-DEPTH DISCOVERY

Resources for students to explore include

- *The 100 Most Difficult Business Letters You'll Ever Have to Write, Fax, or E-Mail* by Bernard Heller. New York: Harperbusiness, 1994. A guide to writing diplomatic and sensitive business letters for every situation in the corporate world.

- *The AMA Handbook of Business Letters* by Jeffrey L. Seglin. New York: AMACOM, 1996. A tool kit for writing effective business correspondence, this book gives guidelines for grammar and style.

- *Business Communication: Process and Product* by Mary Ellen Guffey. Cincinnati, OH: South–Western, 1999. This book combines business situations and business technologies to equip students with communication and career skills.

In the Community

Ask business owners or managers in the community to supply examples of business letters that students may bring to class. Ask students to interview business owners or managers about the kinds of letters they write and the reasons they write them. Ask students to write a paragraph that summarizes what they learned about writing business letters from the business owners or managers.

Job Path Project

Ask students to integrate the material in this unit with their Job Path Projects. Encourage students to think about the kinds of business letters that might be required by the careers they have chosen. Do people in their profession write business letters or proposals? Do people in their professions provide technical information about products?

Discussing the Quote

Ask students to read the quote by Denzel Washington on page 201 of the Student Edition. How does this quote relate to business writing? What might Denzel Washington say about business writing?

Closing the Unit

Bring examples of business letters, proposals, and technical reports to class. Review each type of writing and ask students to identify the distinguishing characteristics of each. What is the purpose of each type of writing? How do the types of writing differ in format? Why is the format of each important? Ask students to suggest three tips for people who are planning to write business letters, proposals, and technical reports. As your students complete each chapter in this unit, you can use the chapter assessments located on the CD-ROM.

Student Edition, pages 202–203

WRITING BUSINESS LETTERS
English in Context

TEACHING THE CHAPTER OPENER

Ms. Willis wants to promote James to manager and put him in charge of his own store. When Ms. Willis asked James to write a letter to one of their suppliers, James was unsure about how to begin. As James and your students will learn, writing business letters is an important job skill and an important method of communication among businesses. In this chapter, students will study the techniques and conventions of letter writing and gain the confidence to write a business letter.

• Ask students to brainstorm the different purposes for business letters. Why are there different types of business letters? What audiences might a business letter target? Write students' ideas on the chalkboard.

PORTFOLIO SETUP: WRITING A BUSINESS LETTER

• On page 227 of the Student Edition, students are asked to write a business letter. Ask students to think of a product they enjoy using. Then, ask students to suppose that they work for the company that makes that product. Ask students to write business letters to inform a customer about the product. Ask students to keep this assignment in mind as they read this chapter. Suggest that they write down ideas for this letter as they think of them.

CD-ROM TEAMWORK/COOPERATIVE ACTIVITY

• This exercise asks a group of students to work together to write several different business letters for a company they work for. The exercise lists a set of issues and asks each student to choose one of them to write about. When students have completed their letters, you may wish to ask them to edit each other's work.

LESSON PLANNING CHART

CHAPTER 10	STUDENT EDITION PAGES	TEACHER'S RESOURCE MANUAL PAGES	CD-ROM
Writing/Reading Activities	207, 209, 210, 214, 218, 221, 224–227	87, 88, 90, 91, 93–95	✓
Speaking/Listening Activities	207, 209, 224	87, 89, 91, 93	✓
Career Activities	209, 214, 226, 227	87, 89, 91	✓
Critical Thinking Activities	204, 208, 209, 211, 214, 215, 219, 220, 222, 226, 227	87–89, 92, 93, 95	✓
Vocabulary Activities	203, 226		✓
ESL/LEP Tips		88, 93, 95	
Teamwork/Cooperative Activities	207, 209, 224	87, 89, 91	✓
Curriculum Connections		92	
Technology Activities	225	92, 116	

LESSON 10-1

Reading Business Letters
Student Edition, pages 204–207

LEARNING OBJECTIVE

▶ Students will learn how to read different kinds of business letters.

Lesson Resources

On the CD-ROM

- Topic at-a-Glance: Reading Business Letters
- Application: Reading Business Letters

In the Handbook

- Reading Strategies: 332–336

INTO
Using Prior Knowledge
Write *request, inform,* and *persuade* on the chalkboard. How are these terms important in business-letter writing? Ask students to list the kinds of business letters that might fall into each category. Then, ask students to preview the lesson headings and captions and predict what they will learn about reading business letters.

THROUGH
Developing the Lesson
Students learn how to recognize different kinds of business letters, which include letters that request, letters that inform, and letters that persuade. They also learn a strategy for reading business letters. Students learn to preview the letter and identify the writer's purpose, to read actively, to pay attention to difficult terms, and to review what they have learned from the letter.

Discussing Visuals Review Figure 10-1, *Writing in the Real World: Business Letter*, on page 205 of the Student Edition. Discuss the callouts with your students. Review Figures 10-2, 10-3, and 10-4 on pages 206 and 207 of the Student Edition. What is the purpose of each of these letters? What is the difference between the appearance of a letter that persuades and one that makes a request?

BEYOND
Closing the Lesson
After students complete the *Apply What You Learn* activity, ask them to reread the letter using the reading strategy outlined in this lesson. How might they improve the letter? Is there anything they would change? Why?

ESL/LEP TIP
Ask students to review the steps of the reading strategy outlined in this lesson with English-proficient students. Are there any steps that are unclear? Ask students to write down the purpose of each step. Then, ask students to practice using the reading strategy.

Extending the Lesson
Ask students to review the business letters that they brought to class for the *In the Community* activity on page 86 of this Teacher's Resource Manual. Ask students to think about how the appearance of each of the letters affects the message the authors want to convey. Ask students to think about the differences in format between a letter that requests, a letter that informs, and a letter that persuades. Why are these differences in format important?

Additional Resource
From Globe Fearon

- *Globe Exercise Books*
  Paragraphs: 36–39

Finding Your Customers and Clients

Student Edition, pages 208–209

INTO

Using Prior Knowledge

Ask students to think about occasions when they were customers or employees. What attracted them to the business or service? Why did they shop or work there? Tell students to put themselves in the place of businesspeople trying to run a successful business. How would they find their customers? Ask students to preview the lesson headings and captions and predict what they will learn about finding customers and clients.

THROUGH

Developing the Lesson

Students learn who their clients and customers are. Then, they learn how to find customers and clients through marketing. They learn that marketing their business involves analyzing the market, checking the competition, and creating a marketing plan. They also learn that a marketing plan may include advertising, direct mailing, and flyers. Review the lists under *Clients* and *Customers* on page 208 of the Student Edition. How would students find customers and clients for each of these businesses?

BEYOND

Closing the Lesson

After students complete the *Apply What You Learn* activity, ask them to suppose they work for a marketing firm. Ask each group to share its marketing plan as if it were presenting the campaign to its client (the class). Ask the class to critique each group's plan. How does the marketing plan attract customers and clients? How can the plan be improved?

Extending the Lesson

Contact and invite a sales and marketing professional to speak to the class about what the profession entails, including what the work is like, what the pay range is, and how students interested in this field can become involved. Check the Yellow Pages under "Marketing" for the names of companies that specialize in this area. Before the guest arrives, ask students to formulate a list of questions to ask the guest speaker. After the presentation, ask students to write business letters thanking the guest.

Grammar Workshop

TIP

Irregular verbs do not follow a predictable pattern. Explain to students that even though they will have to memorize these verbs, they are already familiar with many of them.

Lesson Resources

On the *CD-ROM*

- Grammar Workshop Practice: Using Irregular Verbs
- Grammar Workshop Test: Using Irregular Verbs
- Handbook Practice: Irregular Verbs

In the *Handbook*

- Verb Tense: 352–353

Additional Resources From Globe Fearon:

- *Globe Exercise Books*
  Parts of Speech: 14–15

- *Success in Writing*
  Grammar Skills for Writers: 48–49

USING IRREGULAR VERBS

Grammar Workshop at-a-Glance

This Grammar Workshop focuses on identifying irregular verbs and using them correctly in a sentence.

Error Alert: Solving the Problem

- Write this sentence on the chalkboard: *I throwed out the old files.*
- Ask students, *Is this sentence correct?* (no)
- Ask students, *How can we rewrite this sentence so that it is correct?* (I threw out the old files.)
- Tell students, *Let's look at the list of past participles on page 210 of the Student Edition. What is the past participle of* throw*?*
- Ask students, *How can we rewrite this sentence using the past participle of* throw*?* (I have thrown out the old files.)
- Write this sentence on the chalkboard: *I has taked the work home.*
- Ask students, *Is this sentence correct?* (no)
- Ask students, *How can we rewrite this sentence so that it is correct?* (I have taken work home.)

Write these sentences on the chalkboard. Ask students to rewrite each sentence by first using the past tense verb and then by using *has* or *have* and the past participle.

1. We roded to the office party. (rode, have ridden)

2. I choosed the florist with the quickest service. (chose, have chosen)

3. The staff have spoked to the entrepreneurs about their home office needs. (spoke, has spoken)

4. While you was away, these orders come in. (were, have been; came, have come)

5. The hostess wroted down our order. (wrote, has written)

6. She have taken all her vacation days at once. (took, has taken)

7. They sent the shipment before I am ready to accept it. (was, had been)

8. The company has growed significantly in the past five years. (grew, has grown)

9. The talented marketing firm have catched the eye of our director. (caught, has caught)

10. She has did all her work for the week. (did, has done)

LESSON 10-3

Types of Business Letters

Student Edition, pages 211–214

LEARNING OBJECTIVE

▶ Students will learn different reasons for writing business letters.

Lesson Resource

 On the CD-ROM

- Topic at-a-Glance: Types of Business Letters

INTO

Using Prior Knowledge

Write the words *order letter, request letter, claim letter,* and *adjustment letter* on the chalkboard. Ask students to suggest what each term refers to. Write students' answers on the chalkboard. When you have completed the lesson, review students' answers so that they can see how closely they were able to predict the meanings of these terms. Ask students to preview the lesson headings and captions and predict what they will learn about the different types of business letters.

THROUGH

Developing the Lesson

This lesson introduces students to the order letter, the request letter, the claim letter, and the adjustment letter. They learn how the letters differ and strategies for how to write them. This lesson also addresses written responses to an order letter and a request letter.

Discussing Visuals Review Figure 10-5 on page 211 of the Student Edition. What makes this an order letter? Does it contain all the items that every order letter should contain? Review Figure 10-6, *Writing in the Real World: Request Letter*, on page 213 of the Student Edition. What makes this a persuasive letter?

BEYOND

Closing the Lesson

Ask each student to exchange the letter he or she wrote for the *Apply What You Learn* activity with a classmate. Ask students to write response letters that answer their classmates' letters.

Extending the Lesson

Ask students to form pairs and practice writing one of the types of business letters that they did not choose for the *Apply What You Learn* activity. Tell students that one person in the pair should write one type of letter while the other writes a different type of letter. Then, ask partners to exchange their work and write a response letter that answers the partner's letter.

Job Path Project

Ask students to brainstorm the kinds of compliments and the kinds of complaints a manager in the field of their career choice might receive. Then, ask them to suppose that they are managers in the fields of their career choice and that they just received letters complimenting their company for its service or product. Ask students to write a letter that responds to the compliment. Then, ask students to write a response letter that addresses a complaint.

Determining the Letter Style

Student Edition, pages 215–218

LEARNING OBJECTIVES

▶ Students will learn to create professional-looking business letters.

Lesson Resource

 On the *CD-ROM*

• Topic at-a-Glance: Determining the Letter Style

INTO

Using Prior Knowledge

Bring samples of business letters to class. Ask students to comment on the differences in the style, or appearance, of the letters. How are the letters alike? How are they different? Then, ask students to preview the lesson headings and captions and predict what they will learn about determining letter styles.

THROUGH

Developing the Lesson

Students learn the different types of business letter styles, including block style, modified-block style, and indented style. Students learn that block style is the most common style, modified-block style is less formal than block style, and indented style is the least formal. Students learn how to address a business envelope and how to fold and insert a letter.

Discussing Visuals Review Figures 10-7 and 10-9, *Writing in the Real World: Modified Block-Style*, on pages 215 and 217 of the Student Edition. Which style is each letter written in? Ask students how they can tell. Ask students to rewrite one of these letters, putting it in a form that is different from the one in which it appears.

BEYOND

Closing the Lesson

Ask students to refer to the letters they wrote for the *Apply What You Learn* activity. Ask students to think about why they thought one letter looked better than the other. Was the information easier to read? Did one style look neater than the other?

Curriculum Connection: Social Studies

Ask students to bring examples of business letters from their native countries to class. Ask them to explain to the class how the business-letter styles discussed in Lesson 10-4 are similar to and different from those in their native countries.

Web Activity

Tell students that there are Web sites that offer advice on writing business letters. The Web site from the University of Illinois offers resources for business writers and lists sites that offer help writing business letters, at the following address:
www.english.uiuc.edu/cws/wworkshop/ww_tech.html

Writing for Results
Student Edition, pages 219–220

LEARNING OBJECTIVE

▶ Students will learn tech-niques for writing effective business letters.

INTO
Using Prior Knowledge
Ask students to suppose they are business owners who received a business letter that was negative and did not give any information about its specific complaint. Do they expect this kind of letter to get their attention? Why or why not? What kinds of things should a letter include in order for it to be effective? Ask students to pre-view the lesson headings and captions and predict what they will learn about writing for results.

THROUGH
Developing the Lesson
This lesson focuses on writing an effective letter that will get results. Students learn that the best business letters use simple language and are direct and easy to understand. They learn why it is important to keep the letter positive, how to express empathy toward the person they are writing to, and how to be persuasive. As you read this lesson, ask students to identify other examples of the points discussed in the lesson. What is an example of simple language? What is an example of language that is too complex?

BEYOND
Closing the Lesson
Ask students to refer to the rules that they listed for the *Apply What You Learn* activity. How did they compile the list of rules? Did they use their personal experiences to identify the kinds of things a good complaint department should address?

ESL/LEP Tip
Tone is a difficult topic for many students learning English. Students can practice how to tell when the tone of a letter is angry or sarcastic. Ask these students to write a letter of complaint. Then, ask an English-proficient student to review each sentence with the students and help them adjust the tone accordingly. Are students using the passive voice instead of the active voice? Do their letters express empathy toward the recipient?

Extending the Lesson
Ask students to discuss the experiences they have had when returning items or complaining to stores. Then, tell students to suppose they are working in a store. Ask them to choose one of the complaints that was mentioned during the class discussion and write a letter responding to it. How would students have handled the complaint?

Grammar Workshop

USING BUSINESS TERMS CORRECTLY

Grammar Workshop at-a-Glance

In this Grammar Workshop, students learn some of the most common terms in business and the words that may be confused with them. Examples include *personnel* and *personal* and *stationery* and *stationary*.

Error Alert: Solving the Problem

- Write this sentence on the chalkboard: *The trainee sought (counsel, council) from her mentor.*
- Ask students, *Does anyone know which word is correct?* (counsel)
- Ask students, *Think back to the devices you thought of in Chapter 9. Can you think of a mnemonic device for counsel and council?* (Think of the *i* in council as the *I* for one of the people who is part of the group that gives advice.)
- Write this sentence on the chalkboard: *Information, like age and salary, are (personal, personnel) and confidential.*
- Ask students, *Can you think of a mnemonic device for* personal *and* personnel? (Look at *persona**l*** as *pal* and remember that you only tell private things to your pal.)
- Ask students, *Using our new device, which answer is correct?* (personal)
- Ask students, *What devices can you think of for* principal *and* principle? *For* stationary *and* stationery? (Link the *e* in *stationery* to the *e* in *pen.* You use a pen to write on stationery.)

 Write these sentences on the chalkboard. Ask students to rewrite each sentence using the correct term.

1. The chef is the (*principal*, principle) reason for the restaurant's success.

2. Army (personal, *personnel*) are to check in equipment before more is ordered.

3. The office (stationary, *stationery*) is in that box.

4. The lawyer promised to give (council, *counsel*) and advice.

5. The director of John's gym ordered five new (*stationary*, stationery) bicycles.

Revising Business Letters

Student Edition, pages 222–224

LEARNING OBJECTIVE

▶ Students will learn how to revise a business letter for content and organization.

Lesson Resource

 On the CD-ROM

• Topic at-a-Glance: Revising Business Letters

INTO

Using Prior Knowledge

Students may remember the guidelines for revising from other lessons in the book. Ask them to recall as many details as they can about what writers do when they revise their work. Write their answers on the chalkboard. Then, ask students to preview the lesson headings and captions and predict what they will learn about revising business letters.

THROUGH

Developing the Lesson

This lesson teaches students how to edit and proofread their letters. Students learn how to edit for content and for organization. They learn that editing for content means assessing the clarity of their letters. Then, they learn that editing for organization means checking for style and making sure that their letters have introductory paragraphs, bodies that state the main points, and closing paragraphs. Students learn that peer editing is an effective way to check letters for content and organization. Finally, students learn that proofreading for mechanics, grammar, and spelling gives letters their polished, professional look.

Discussing Visuals Review Figure 10-11 on page 223 of the Student Edition. How might the questions in this chart help students to revise a letter?

BEYOND

Closing the Lesson

Ask students to use the checklist that they created for the *Apply What You Learn* activity to edit a letter they wrote for a previous lesson in this chapter. Students might also exchange letters with each other and edit them using the checklist. How did the checklist help them edit the letters? What kinds of errors were students able to identify using the checklist that they may otherwise have missed?

ESL/LEP Tip

Students learning English may not understand all of the different editing and proofreading terms in this lesson. Ask English-proficient students to briefly explain what each term means so that they can correct any misconceptions. Then, ask students to create a checklist that explains troublesome editing and proofreading terms in their native languages as well as in English.

Additional Resource From Globe Fearon:

• *Globe Exercise Books*
  Paragraphs: 26–33

Student Edition, pages 228–229

WRITING A PROPOSAL TO SOLVE PROBLEMS

English in Context

TEACHING THE CHAPTER OPENER

John is an employee with an idea. He works in the mailroom and has come up with a way to improve how the mail is sorted. What he doesn't know is how to write a proposal to his boss that will explain his idea. Proposals, what they are, and how to write them are the topic of this chapter. These lessons help students understand the process of writing proposals by providing students with the opportunity to practice writing their own.

• Ask students what a proposal is. Write their answers on the chalkboard. Then, write the word *propose* on the board and tell students that the word *proposal* is in the same word family. Ask students the meaning of *propose,* which is "to suggest." Then, explain to students that making a suggestion is what a proposal does.

PORTFOLIO SETUP: WRITING A PROPOSAL

• On page 253 of the Student Edition, students are asked to write a proposal. You may wish to introduce the Portfolio Project at the beginning of this chapter so students have time to think about both a problem and a solution for their writing assignment.

CD-ROM TEAMWORK/COOPERATIVE ACTIVITY

• This activity asks groups to create a proposal for improving the cafeteria at their school. Each group assigns researchers to investigate problems, writers to gather information to support the researchers' conclusions, and designers to use graphics and illustrations to design a proposal.

LESSON PLANNING CHART			
CHAPTER 11	**STUDENT EDITION PAGES**	**TEACHER'S RESOURCE MANUAL PAGES**	**CD-ROM**
Writing/Reading Activities	234, 235, 239, 243, 248, 250, 252, 253	96–105	✓
Speaking/Listening Activities	232, 234, 239, 250	96, 98, 100, 103	✓
Career Activities	251, 253	101	✓
Critical Thinking Activities	230, 233, 236, 240, 242, 244, 247, 249, 250, 252, 253	97, 98, 100, 101, 103, 105	✓
Vocabulary Activities	229, 252		✓
ESL/LEP Tips		97	
Teamwork/Cooperative Activities	232, 234, 250	96, 100, 103	✓
Curriculum Connections		97, 98	
Technology Activities	251	101, 103, 116	✓

Reading Proposals

Student Edition, pages 230–232

LEARNING OBJECTIVE

▶ Students will learn to recognize and read a proposal.

Lesson Resources

On the *CD-ROM*

• Graphic Organizer: Using the KWL Chart

In the *Handbook*

• Reading Strategies: 332–336

INTO

Using Prior Knowledge

Ask students how they solve problems that they encounter at school or at work. Discuss students' suggestions. Then, explain that one common way to effect change or solve problems in business is to write a proposal. Ask students to preview the lesson headings and captions and predict what they will learn about reading proposals.

THROUGH

Developing the Lesson

Students learn that a proposal is a written plan of action in business. It can be written within a company to improve it or by a supplier who wants to do business with the company. Students learn that there are brief proposals, such as a quote or a request for proposal, as well as lengthier proposals. Students also learn that a proposal includes a cover letter, a title page, a table of contents, an executive summary, a current situation section, a recommended solution section, a cost and timetable section, and an appendix. Finally, students learn the KWL reading strategy for reading proposals.

Discussing Visuals Review Figure 11-1 on page 232 of the Student Edition. Discuss how students can use the KWL strategy to read a proposal. Why is the KWL strategy useful when reading a proposal?

BEYOND

Closing the Lesson

Ask students to refer to the problems their group addressed in the *Apply What You Learn* activity. How would a proposal help this problem? Then, ask students to review the list of people, products, or services that might help solve the problem. How are the people, products, or services they listed important to the proposal?

ESL/LEP Tip

Ask students to work with English-proficient students to review words and concepts such as *proposal; quote; RFP, or request for proposal; executive summary; current situation; recommended solution; cost and timetable;* and *appendix.* Where do these sections appear in a proposal?

Curriculum Connection: Social Studies

Ask students to research the grant-seeking process at a nonprofit group in their community. Tell students that they can conduct their research on the phone or in person. How do nonprofit groups prepare proposals to acquire funding? new equipment?

Additional Resources
From Globe Fearon:

• *Be a Better Reader*
  Level A: 114
  Level D: 30

• *Reading in the Content Areas*
  Level A: 4–7
  Level B: 12–15
  Level D: 4–7

• *Writer's Toolkit*
  Gathering Details: KWL Chart

Analyzing the Problem
Student Edition, pages 233–234

LEARNING OBJECTIVE

▶ Students will learn how to analyze a work-related problem.

INTO
Using Prior Knowledge
Ask students to suppose that they work for a window manufacturing company. Customers are often frustrated because the order form they must fill out is long and complicated. They tell the student-employees that they never want to do business with the company again. What should the students do? Ask students to brainstorm possible solutions. Then, ask students to preview the lesson headings and captions and predict what they will learn about analyzing problems.

THROUGH
Developing the Lesson
Students learn how to recognize that a problem exists, how to make a plan to solve the problem, how to analyze an RFP, how to know customers' expectations, and how to brainstorm a plan. Divide students into groups, and give each group a hypothetical situation to solve. Possible situations include a pizza store losing money because another pizza store opened across the street, a bookstore losing customers to Internet retailers, or a toy manufacturer's best-seller is suddenly not popular.

- Is the situation a problem? Why or why not?
- What is needed to solve the problem?
- What are the customers' expectations?
- What ideas can they brainstorm to solve the problem?

BEYOND
Closing the Lesson
Ask students to think about the solutions they brainstormed for the *Apply What You Learn* activity. Then, ask them to explain why they chose the solutions they did. Did they use the questions listed above?

Curriculum Connection: Science
The process of developing inventions often begins with a need or a problem the inventor is trying to solve. Ask students to research a famous invention to learn the process by which the inventor reached a solution. Then, ask students to write two to three paragraphs that describe the process. How is it similar to the method of solving problems described in this lesson?

Grammar Workshop

TIP

Explain to students that when they quote something, they state exactly what a person said or wrote. Tell them that quotations show another person's ideas and add excitement to writing.

Lesson Resources

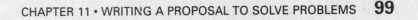 **On the CD-ROM**

- Grammar Workshop Practice: Using Quotation Marks Correctly
- Grammar Workshop Test: Using Quotation Marks Correctly
- Handbook Practice: Quotation Marks

In the Handbook

- Quotation Marks: 360

Additional Resources From Globe Fearon:

- *Globe Exercise Books* Punctuation: 6–7
- *Success in Writing* Grammar Skills for Writers: 76–77

USING QUOTATION MARKS CORRECTLY

Grammar Workshop at-a-Glance

This Grammar Workshop teaches students a variety of ways to use quotations. Students learn that quotation marks are used to set off direct speech, to highlight slang terms, and to set off titles of songs, poems, short stories, lectures, radio and television episodes, chapters of books, magazine and newspaper articles, slogans, and encyclopedia entries.

Error Alert: Solving the Problem

- Write this sentence on the chalkboard: *Okay, everyone, said the store manager, we open in ten minutes.*

- Ask students, *Is this sentence correct? Is anything missing?* ("Okay, everyone," said the store manager, "We open in ten minutes.")

- Write this sentence on the chalkboard: *I told Donna, We are expecting a large party, and she prepared extra place settings.*

- Ask students, *Is this sentence correct? Is anything missing?* ("I told Donna, 'We are expecting a large party,' and she prepared extra place settings.")

- Write this sentence on the chalkboard: *I read Chapter 9, which is titled The Committee Welcomed Him Home.*

- Ask students, *Is this sentence correct? Is anything missing?* (I read Chapter 9, which is titled "The Committee Welcomed Him Home.")

✏ Write these sentences on the chalkboard. Ask students to use quotation marks where needed.

1. I read the article titled Make Your Minutes Count.

2. Making Business Count was the name of the article, wasn't it? he asked.

3. His lecture, Seven Mistakes You Are Making With Your Customers, was a hit with our sales staff, said Mr. Parker.

4. The radio broadcast, Financial Future, was on public radio, he told us.

5. Her short story, Time for the Office, told about her time at BestStar, Jim explained.

Developing a Strategy
Student Edition, pages 236–239

LEARNING OBJECTIVE

▶ Students will learn how to develop a strategy to solve a problem.

Lesson Resource

On the *CD-ROM*

• Application: Developing a Strategy

INTO
Using Prior Knowledge
Ask students to suppose that they work at a new convenience store. There is nothing on the shelves, and the manager has asked them to stock the store. How do they decide what to put where? How could a strategy help students solve this problem? Ask students to preview the lesson headings and captions and predict what they will learn about developing a strategy.

THROUGH
Developing the Lesson
In this lesson, students learn that a strategy is used to solve a problem. They learn that a *strategy statement* proposes a solution. The lesson gives students a checklist that helps them to develop their strategy into a proposal. Then, students learn to think through their strategy by responding to each of the questions on the checklist. Students also learn how to decide if a strategy will work by comparing it to another strategy.

Discussing Visuals Review Figure 11-2 on page 237 of the Student Edition. Discuss the importance of each question. How can the questions on this checklist help explore a strategy? Review Figure 11-3, *Writing in the Real World: Strategy Statements*, on page 238 of the Student Edition. Discuss the differences between the two strategy statements. Why is it important to use the best strategy?

BEYOND
Closing the Lesson
Ask students to exchange the strategies they wrote for the *Apply What You Learn* activity with a classmate. Does their classmate's statement address all of the questions on the checklist? How is their strategy better than Strategy 1 and Strategy 2 on page 238 of the Student Edition?

Extending the Lesson
Ask students to form groups and use the method in this lesson to formulate a solution to a problem their school faces. Possible problems are bad food in the cafeteria, not enough parking, too many cliques, or too few athletic opportunities. Ask each group to work through the strategy questions and answer each of them. Then, ask each group to present the problem and strategy to the class. Ask the students to imagine that they are administrators. Would the strategy presented by the group convince them to do something about the problem? What could the group have added to make its strategy seem more effective?

Additional Resources
From Globe Fearon:

• *Globe Exercise Books*
  Paragraphs: 20–21

• *Be a Better Reader*
  Level B: 29–30
  Level C: 172–173
  Level G: 170–171

• *Writer's Toolkit*
  Gathering Details: Venn Diagram

Collecting Supporting Information

Student Edition, pages 240–242

LEARNING OBJECTIVE

▶ Students will learn how to collect supporting information to write a proposal.

Lesson Resource

On the CD-ROM

• Application: Collecting Supporting Information

INTO

Using Prior Knowledge

Ask students to imagine that they are employed by an a office supplies store. Their boss has asked them to write a proposal to another company because he wants to become its exclusive supplier of office supplies. What information would they need to write an effective proposal and persuade the other company? Ask students to preview the lesson headings and captions and predict what they will learn about collecting supporting information.

THROUGH

Developing the Lesson

Students learn the importance of research and the significance of documentation. They learn that identifying company needs and learning the company culture can be important when researching a proposal. They learn to use the Internet, newspapers, magazines, and surveys as sources of information. They also learn how to form and use focus groups to gather information. Review the sample case on pages 241 and 242 of the Student Edition. What sources did Julie use to compile her report? How is each of them important?

Discussing Visuals Review Figure 11-4 on page 241 of the Student Edition. Review how each source can help someone collect information. What kinds of information would students expect to gather from each of these sources?

BEYOND

Closing the Lesson

Ask students to review the types of information they listed for the *Apply What You Learn* activity. Ask students to explain why they chose those sources. What kind of information do they expect to get from each one? Did they consider any other types of sources, such as customer interviews?

Web Activity

Ask students to use the Internet to complete the Job Path Project on this page. What kinds of information are they able to gather from an Internet search?

Job Path Project

Ask students to imagine that they are writing a proposal to provide or expand a product or service they might be supplying as an employee in their profession. Where can they look for supporting information?

Additional Resources
From Globe Fearon:

• *Success in Writing*
  Writing to Persuade: 26

• *Writer's Toolkit*
  Writing Handbook: Elements of Nonfiction: Using Resources

Grammar Workshop

TIP

Explain to students that they should avoid using slang in the workplace. Tell them that omitting slang from their vocabulary will help them to make an articulate and refined impression on their employer.

Lesson Resources

 On the *CD-ROM*

- Grammar Workshop Practice: Using Appropriate Language
- Grammar Workshop Test: Using Appropriate Language

 In the *Handbook*

- Appropriate Language: 342

USING APPROPRIATE LANGUAGE

Grammar Workshop at-a-Glance

This Grammar Workshop teaches students about language that is appropriate for the workplace.

Error Alert: Solving the Problem

- Write this sentence on the chalkboard: *Get me that list.*

- Ask students, *Does this sound like the correct way to speak to a co-worker or supervisor?* (no)

- Ask students, *How can we rewrite this sentence so that it is appropriate for the workplace?* (Please give me that list.)

- Write this sentence on the chalkboard: *You wanna go to lunch?*

- Ask students, *Does this sound like the correct way to speak to a co-worker or supervisor?* (no)

- Ask students, *How can we rewrite this sentence so that it is appropriate for the workplace?* (Would you like to go to lunch?)

 Write these sentence on the chalkboard. Ask students to rewrite these sentences using formal language.

1. I'm goin' now.

2. You need me to do anything?

3. Whadya mean?

4. I'm leaving early today.

5. When is this thing due?

- Read the following situations to your students. Ask students to generate a way to verbalize each of them using appropriate language.

1. An employee tells a customer that the item cannot be returned because there is no receipt.

2. An employee talks to another employee about a report that one of them was supposed to finish.

3. An employee asks an employer for a vacation day.

4. An employee tells a customer that the store is out of the light bulbs the customer wants to buy.

5. An employee informs an employer about problems with the quality of an order of fresh flowers.

LESSON 11-5

Writing the Proposal
Student Edition, pages 244–247

INTO
Using Prior Knowledge
Ask students to think about the checklists they used and the sources they learned about. How would they compile all of these things to make a proposal? Ask students to identify the steps they would take in writing a proposal. Write their ideas on the chalkboard. Then, ask them to preview the lesson headings and captions, and ask them to predict what they will learn about writing proposals.

THROUGH
Developing the Lesson
This lesson explains the steps involved in writing a proposal. Students learn that first they should determine their purpose and think about their audience. Then, they should make a plan for writing, prepare a first draft, edit the draft, proofread the proposal, and publish the proposal.

Discussing Visuals Review Figure 11-6, *Writing in the Real World: Proposal* on page 246 of the Student Edition. Create a list on the chalkboard of the steps in writing a proposal: determine purpose, determine audience, create a plan for writing, write, edit, proofread, and publish. How does the writer of the proposal in Figure 11-6 address each of these steps?

BEYOND
Closing the Lesson
After students list their three best reasons in the *Apply What You Learn* activity, ask them to write an executive summary. When students have finished their executive summaries, ask them to exchange their work with one another. Then, ask students to critique their classmates' papers and offer suggestions. Does the summary have a purpose? Does it take its audience into consideration? Was the summary edited? proofread?

Web Activity
These Web sites have advice for people who are writing grant proposals. Your students may find them a useful way to get another perspective on the process of writing proposals.
www.teachnet.org/docs/Grants/Howto/index.htm
www.ric.edu/index/htm

Additional Resources From Globe Fearon:

• *Success in Writing*
  Writing to Persuade: 23–25, 30–37

• *Writer's Toolkit*
  Considering Audience and Purpose
  Revising and Editing
  Proofreading
  Handbook: Writing Handbook: The Writing Process: Drafting

Grammar Workshop

TIP

Explain to students that recording numbers accurately can make a tremendous difference for a company. Ask students to imagine what would happen if a customer was supposed to be billed $862.00 but was only billed $86.20? Ask students to think about how consistent errors of this nature might affect a business.

Lesson Resources

🥏 **On the CD-ROM**

• Grammar Workshop Practice: Using Numbers in Context

• Grammar Workshop Test: Using Numbers in Context

📖 **In the Handbook**

• Numbers: 365

Additional Resources From Globe Fearon:

• *Globe Exercise Books*
  Mechanics and Usage: 42–43

• *Success in Writing*
  Grammar Skills for Writers: 82

USING NUMBERS IN CONTEXT

Grammar Workshop at-a-Glance

In this Grammar Workshop, students learn how to write numbers. They learn when they should be written as words and as numerals. They also learn how numbers should be treated when they begin a sentence and when they are combined with words.

Error Alert: Solving the Problem

• Write this sentence on the chalkboard: *The dental hygenist ordered 4 cases of dental floss.*

• Ask students, *Is this sentence correct?* (no; *4* should be *four*)

• Write this sentence on the chalkboard: *The invoice totaled nine hundred fifty dollars.*

• Ask students, *Is this sentence correct?* (no; *nine hundred fifty dollars* should be *$950.00*)

• Write this sentence on the chalkboard: *Feel free to contact customer service at one eight hundred five five five one two one two.*

• Ask students, *Is this sentence correct?* (no; *one eight hundred five five five one two one two* should be *1 (800) 555-1212*)

• Write this sentence on the chalkboard: *The dresser weighs fifty pounds.*

• Ask students, *Is this sentence correct?* (no; *fifty* should be *50 pounds*)

• Write this sentence on the chalkboard: *Park Associates invested $2,000,000.00 in a new facility.*

• Ask students, *Is this sentence correct?* (no; *$2,000,000.00* should be *$2 million*)

✏️ Write these sentences on the chalkboard. Ask students to correct each sentence by correctly rewriting the numbers.

1. The package service mailed six hundred ninety nine packets. (699)

2. On May ninth, four thousand six hundred dentists will attend the conference. (May 9, 4,600)

3. The bill came to thirty-nine dollars and fifty three cents. ($39.53)

4. The box of books weighs ten pounds. (10 pounds)

5. In nineteen hundred and ninety-nine, Draco Corporation reported a profit of ten million dollars. (1999/$10 million)

Using Visuals in a Proposal

Student Edition, pages 249–250

LEARNING OBJECTIVES

▶ Students will learn how to use charts and tables in a proposal.

Lesson Resource

On the CD-ROM

• Application: Using Visuals in a Proposal

INTO

Using Prior Knowledge

Find a dramatic photograph from a magazine or newspaper. Describe it to students, and then show them the photograph. Then, ask whether the verbal description or the actual photograph was more effective in visualizing the scene. What made one more effective than the other? Explain that adding graphics and illustrations to proposals can be very effective. Ask students to preview the lesson headings and captions and predict what they will learn about using visuals in proposals.

THROUGH

Developing the Lesson

Students learn why visuals can be an effective addition to a proposal. Students learn to plan their design by asking themselves a series of questions about their proposals. Then, students learn how to design their proposals by choosing font types and sizes, colors that are easy to read, and illustrations. Finally, students learn how to create and place graphics, tables, and charts.

Discussing Visuals Review Figure 11-7 on page 250 of the Student Edition. Ask students to think about what this information might look like if it was presented in a paragraph. Why is this kind of information easier to read when it is in a table? What other type of graphic could be used to present the same information? What did students take into consideration when deciding on an alternate graphic? Did they consider the space? their audience? the information being presented?

BEYOND

Closing the Lesson

Ask students to explain the reason for each of the improvements they suggested in the *Apply What You Learn* activity. Why did they choose to change the font type? The spacing? The organization of the material? How did they decide on the visuals they chose? Ask students to use the improvements they suggested to redesign the proposal.

Extending the Lesson

Find examples of proposals with graphics and without graphics. Ask students to analyze the proposals without graphics and suggest graphics that could be added to create a more effective report. Where should the visuals be placed? (If you are unable to find two proposals, you can use two articles about the same subject or event and delete the graphics from one of the articles.)

READING AND WRITING TECHNICAL INFORMATION
English in Context

TEACHING THE CHAPTER OPENER

David knows how to operate the canning machine at the juice company where he works. His boss, Mr. Gage, is worried about what will happen if David gets sick or is moved to another machine. Now, Mr. Gage wants him to write a short technical report that explains how to operate the machine. David does not know what a technical report looks like and is unsure about how to approach writing it. This chapter will help students understand how to read and write technical reports.

• Ask students if they would feel comfortable writing a technical report about a piece of machinery they know how to operate, such as a microwave oven or a computer. How would they approach this assignment?

PORTFOLIO SETUP: WRITING A TECHNICAL REPORT

• On page 281 of the Student Edition, students are asked to write a technical report. Students create a new invention or suggest an improvement for a product that already exists. Then, they write a brief technical article that explains the product and how to use it. Students are encouraged to include visuals as part of their reports. Ask students to begin thinking about possible project topics.

CD-ROM TEAMWORK/COOPERATIVE ACTIVITY

• This activity asks a group of students to work together to prepare a technical report that explains how to run a piece of school equipment. Students begin by researching problems that arise when using software, hardware, or power tools. Then, each student in the group chooses to take on the role of researcher, writer, or designer. Ask groups to post their reports near the item they focused on.

LESSON PLANNING CHART

CHAPTER 12	STUDENT EDITION PAGES	TEACHER'S RESOURCE MANUAL PAGES	CD-ROM
Writing/Reading Activities	258, 259, 263, 266, 267, 272, 275, 276, 278–282	106–109, 111–115	✓
Speaking/Listening Activities	263, 271, 276, 278	106, 109, 114	✓
Career Activities	271, 281, 282	112	✓
Critical Thinking Activities	256, 258, 260, 264, 266, 268, 271, 273, 277, 280–282	106, 107, 109, 110, 112, 114, 115	✓
Vocabulary Activities	255, 280	110	✓
ESL/LEP Tips		107, 110, 114	
Teamwork/Cooperative Activities	263, 276	106, 109, 114	✓
Curriculum Connections		110, 115	
Technology Activities	279	114, 116	

Reading Technical Writing
Student Edition, pages 256–258

INTO
Using Prior Knowledge
Ask students what technical writing they have encountered in their daily lives. How would they describe it? What is the purpose of technical writing? Ask students to preview the lesson headings and captions and predict what they will learn about reading technical writing.

THROUGH
Developing the Lesson
Students learn that technical writing explains how a product, idea, or process works. They learn that there are two kinds of technical writing, technical articles and technical reports, and how they differ from one another. Students also learn that there are five main types of technical reports: technical-background reports, instructions, recommendation reports, primary-research reports, and technical specifications. Finally, students learn how to read technical articles and technical reports using the KWL strategy.

Discussing Visuals Review Figure 12-2 on page 257 of the Student Edition. Ask students to think of an example of each type of technical report. Why is it necessary to have five different types of reports? Discuss Figure 12-1 on page 256 of the Student Edition. Ask students what type of technical writing this is. How can they tell?

BEYOND
Closing the Lesson
Once students identify the author's main purpose and the audience for the *Apply What You Learn* activity, ask students to identify the type of technical report they have selected. Then, ask students to give three reasons why they think this is so.

Extending the Lesson
Tell students to refer to the piece of technical writing from the *Apply What You Learn* activity. Ask students to review the reading strategy steps outlined on page 258 of the Student Edition. Then, ask students to use the KWL strategy to help them read through the piece of writing.

ESL/LEP Tip
Ask students to work with English-proficient students to review words and phrases such as *technical writing, manual, trade journal, technical background report, recommendation report, primary-research report, and technical specifications.* Ask students to write a description of each word or phrase to help them to remember their meanings.

LEARNING OBJECTIVE

▶ Students will learn to read different types of technical writing.

Lesson Resources

On the *CD-ROM*
- Topic at-a-Glance: Reading Technical Writing
- Graphic Organizer: Using the KWL Chart

In the *Handbook*
- Reading Strategies: 332–336

Additional Resources
From Globe Fearon:

- *Reading in the Content Areas*
  Level A: 4–7
  Level B: 12–15
  Level D: 4–17

- *Writer's Toolkit*
  Inspirations for Writing: Modes: Practical and Technical Writing; Gathering Details: KWL Chart

---

Grammar Workshop

TIP

Tell students to think carefully about what they are describing before they choose an adjective or an adverb. Explain that visualizing can help them choose the right words and paint a clear picture when writing a résumé or a technical report.

Lesson Resources

On the *CD-ROM*

- Grammar Workshop Practice: Using Adjectives and Adverbs That Compare

- Grammar Workshop Test: Using Adjectives and Adverbs That Compare

- Handbook Practice: Comparative and Superlative Adjectives

- Handbook Practice: Comparative and Superlative Adverbs and Negatives

In the *Handbook*

- Modifiers: 353–355

Additional Resources From Globe Fearon:

- *Globe Exercise Books*
  Parts of Speech: 30–31, 34–35

- *Success in Writing*
  Grammar Skills for Writers: 56

FORMING ADJECTIVES AND ADVERBS THAT COMPARE

Grammar Workshop at-a-Glance

This Grammar Workshop teaches students about comparative and superlative adjectives and adverbs. Students learn that most adjectives or adverbs with one syllable add *-er* or *-est*, most adjectives or adverbs that end in *-y* change the *y* to *i* and add *-er* or *-est*, some adjectives add the words *more* and *most*, and some have irregular forms.

Error Alert: Solving the Problem

- Write this sentence on the chalkboard: *Will the new building be closest than the old one?*

- Ask students, *Is this correct?* (no; *closest* should be *closer*) Ask students, *How could we rewrite this sentence to show that the new building will be closer than all four buildings?* (Will the new building be the closest?)

- Write this sentence on the chalkboard: *He could not have gotten there any early!*

- Ask students, *Is this correct?* (no; *early* should be *earlier*) Ask students, *How could we rewrite this sentence to show that he arrived before everyone else?* (He was the earliest to arrive.)

- Write this sentence on the chalkboard: *The new vendor was efficienter than the one we used in the past.*

- Ask students, *Is this correct?* (no; *efficienter* should be *more efficient*) Ask students, *How could we rewrite this sentence to show that the new vendor is more efficient than any other vendor?* (The new vendor was the most efficient one we ever used.)

Write these sentences on the chalkboard. Ask students to rewrite each sentence and correct the adjective or the adverb.

1. Restaurant Blanc was the nicer place Adriana ever worked. (nicest)

2. The first ad campaign was funniest than the second. (funnier)

3. Doris had the supportivist supervisor. (most supportive)

4. The second interviewer offered Joanna a more good job. (better)

5. The summer internship offered Gary the goodest job opportunity he ever had. (best)

Organizing Technical Writing

Student Edition, pages 260–263

LEARNING OBJECTIVE

▶ Students will learn how to use patterns of organization in technical writing.

Lesson Resources

On the CD-ROM

- Topic at-a-Glance: Organizing Technical Writing
- Application: Organizing Technical Writing
- Various Graphic Organizers

In the Handbook

- Strategies for Organizing Your Writing: 338–339

Additional Resources From Globe Fearon:

- *Globe Exercise Books* *Paragraphs*: 16–19

- *Success in Writing* *Grammar Skills for Writers*: 100–101

- *Writer's Toolkit* Organizing Details: Timeline, Chain of Events Handbook: Writing Handbook: Elements of Nonfiction: Factual Information

INTO

Using Prior Knowledge

Ask students to do a simple task, such as sharpening a pencil or arranging their books in a certain way. However, make your directions as disorganized as possible. When you have finished, ask students what they thought of your explanation. Explain to students that their frustration is what a reader experiences when technical writing is not thoughtfully organized. Ask students if they have read technical writing that was confusing. Then, ask students to preview the lesson headings and captions and predict what they will learn about organizing technical writing.

THROUGH

Developing the Lesson

Students learn how to apply the writing process to technical writing. They learn to select a topic, consider purpose and audience, evaluate sources of information, and select an organizational pattern. They learn to ask important questions about their audience. They also learn that they can organize their reports using chronological order, spatial order, cause-and-effect order, whole-to-parts order, or parts-to-whole order.

Discussing Visuals Review Figure 12-4, *Writing in the Real World: A Technical Report*, on page 262 of the Student Edition. Discuss the callouts. How is the organizational method used effectively? What other method can be used? Ask students to explain their answers.

BEYOND

Closing the Lesson

Ask each pair of students to choose an organizational method for the topic they chose for the *Apply What You Learn* activity. Tell students to take into consideration the topics they are writing about and the kind of supporting information they evaluated in the *Apply What You Learn* activity. Ask students to explain why they choose a particular method.

Extending the Lesson

Ask students to bring to class examples of technical writing that they have encountered at school, at home, or on the job. Ask students to identify the method used to organize their examples of technical writing. How does this organizational method present the information in a useful manner? What other method might improve the presentation of information?

LEARNING OBJECTIVES

▶ Students will learn how to write a lab report.

Lesson Resource

On the CD-ROM

• Topic at-a-Glance: Writing Lab Reports

Writing Lab Reports

Student Edition, pages 264–266

INTO

Using Prior Knowledge

Ask students if they have ever conducted a science experiment. How did they report the results of the experiment? How was that report different from other writing they have done? Ask students to think about the kind of information their report included. What was the most effective way to organize it? Ask students to preview the lesson headings and captions and predict what they will learn about writing lab reports.

THROUGH

Developing the Lesson

Students learn that lab reports detail how an experiment is conducted and the results. They learn how to plan a lab report by thinking about their audience, keeping their descriptions short and clear, and using formal language. This lesson gives students suggestions for writing the abstract, introduction, materials, procedure, results, discussion, and references sections of a lab report.

Discussing Visuals Review Figure 12-6, *Writing in the Real World: Lab Report*, on page 265 of the Student Edition. Discuss the callouts. Why is this format suitable for the information it is presenting? How does this format make the information easy to read? Why is each section of the lab report important?

BEYOND

Closing the Lesson

After students describe the audience for and the purpose of the lab report in Figure 12-6 on page 265 of the Student Edition for the *Apply What You Learn* activity, ask students to respond to the descriptions and the language. Are the descriptions short and clear? Is the language formal? Ask students to give examples of the short and clear descriptions and the formal language. Why are the results presented as a graphic?

ESL/LEP Tip

Ask English-proficient students to work with students to define common lab report terms, such as *abstract, procedure, observations, experiment,* and *hypothesis.* Ask students to write a definition for each of these terms that will help them to remember their meanings.

Curriculum Connection: Science

Ask a science teacher at your school to recommend a simple experiment that you can conduct in your classroom. Ask students to work in groups to complete the experiment and write a lab report.

Grammar Workshop

TIP

Tell students that sometimes the indefinite pronoun contains a clue that can help them determine agreement. For example, a word like *everyone* contains the word *one* and takes a singular verb.

Lesson Resources

💿 On the *CD-ROM*

- Grammar Workshop Practice: Indefinite Pronouns and Agreement
- Grammar Workshop Test: Indefinite Pronouns and Agreement

📖 In the *Handbook*

- Pronouns: 350–351

INDEFINITE PRONOUNS AND AGREEMENT

Grammar Workshop at-a-Glance

This Grammar Workshop focuses on indefinite pronouns. Students learn that singular indefinite pronouns, such as *another, anybody, anyone, each, either, everybody, everyone, everything, neither, nobody, none, no one, nothing, one, other, somebody, someone,* and *something* require singular verbs. Plural indefinite pronouns, such as *all, both, few, many, most, others, several,* and *some* require plural verbs.

Error Alert: Solving the Problem

- Write this sentence on the chalkboard: *No one go out for lunch.*

- Ask students, *Is this correct?* (No; *go* should be *goes.*)

- Write this sentence on the chalkboard: *Everyone (contribute) to the company's success.*

- Ask students, *How can we write this sentence so that the verb form agrees with the indefinite pronoun?* (Everyone contributes to the company's success.)

- Write this sentence on the chalkboard: *Both of them is hard workers.*

- Ask students, *Is this correct?* (No; *is* should be *are.*)

- Write this sentence on the chalkboard: *Many has to attend.*

- Ask students, *How can we rewrite this sentence so that the verb form agrees with the indefinite pronoun?* (Many have to attend.)

- Write this sentence on the chalkboard: *Somebody know what everybody are doing.*

- Ask students, *Is this correct?* (no; *know* should be *knows* and *are* should be *is*)

- ✏️ Write these sentences on the chalkboard. Ask students to rewrite each sentence so that the verb form agrees with the indefinite pronoun.

  1. Few (know) about the change. (know)

  2. One of the customers (finish) the report. (finishes)

  3. Many (speak) highly of her work. (speak)

  4. No one, except Mr. James, (agree) with the conclusion. (agrees)

  5. Many students (volunteer) as interns at Willow, Inc. (volunteer)

Additional Resource From Globe Fearon:

- *Globe Exercise Books*
  Mechanics and Usage: 22–23

Writing Progress Reports

Student Edition, pages 268–271

INTO

Using Prior Knowledge

Ask students to think about a project they are working on at home, at school, or on the job. How might they communicate the progress they are making on their project? What kind of information would their report include? Ask students to preview the lesson headings and captions and predict what they will learn about writing progress reports.

THROUGH

Developing the Lesson

Students learn that progress reports, which are made up of the heading, introduction, background, work completed, work underway, problems, work scheduled, and conclusion sections, provide important information about a project. They can explain how much work has been completed, how much work is being done, how much work remains to be done, and what unexpected problems have developed. The lesson also explains how to write a progress report and includes a checklist that students can use.

Discussing Visuals Review Figure 12-9, *Writing in the Real World: Progress Report*, on page 270 of the Student Edition. Discuss the callouts. Why is this format suitable for the information it is presenting? How is each section of the progress report important?

BEYOND

Closing the Lesson

After students complete the *Apply What You Learn* activity, ask them to write a progress report that explains the progress they made completing this activity. Ask students to consider the format that they will use for their reports. Should they present their information in the form of a memo? a letter? Then, ask them to use the checklist and report on the research they did for the *Apply What You Learn* activity.

Job Path Project

Ask students to use the progress report format to assess the progress they are making with their Job Path Projects. Ask students to address each of the sections of a progress report by considering the following: the heading; introduction (What career are they researching?); background (Why did they choose to research this career?); work completed (To date, what have they done for their Job Path Project?); work underway (What they are currently working on?); problems (What problems have they encountered?); work scheduled (What do they plan to do to complete their Job Path Project?); and conclusion (What have they learned so far?).

Grammar Workshop

-

USING HYPHENS CORRECTLY IN COMPOUND WORDS

Grammar Workshop at-a-Glance

This Grammar Workshop focuses on using hyphens to join the parts of compound words, compound numbers, a person's age, and fractions and to form new words that start with *self-*, *all-*, *half-*, or *great-*.

Error Alert: Solving the Problem

- Write this sentence on the chalkboard: *At the annual company picnic, José and Jeff participated in the four legged race.*
- Ask students, *Is this correct?* (No; *four legged* should be *four-legged*.)
- Write this sentence on the chalkboard: *Every new employee receives on the job training.*
- Ask students, *Is this correct?* (No; *on the job* should be *on-the-job*.)
- Write this sentence on the chalkboard: *Grace always seems so self confident.*
- Ask students, *Is this correct?* (No; *self confident* should be *self-confident*.)

Write these sentences on the chalkboard. Ask students to correct each sentence by properly inserting the hyphens.

1. Tira is editor in chief at the magazine. (editor-in-chief)
2. Cameron has been with the company for twenty nine years. (twenty-nine)
3. Last month, sales were at an all time high. (all-time)
4. The bridal shop received a new shipment of mother of the bride dresses. (mother-of-the-bride)
5. Eight hundred ninety three people responded to Research Inc.'s survey. (Eight hundred ninety-three)

TIP

Tell students that when two words are combined to describe a noun, they should ask whether the description comes before the noun or after the noun. Explain that they should use a hyphen when the description comes before the noun. For example: *They have a strong-willed team.* Students should not use a hyphen if the description comes after the noun. For example: *Their team is strong willed.*

Lesson Resources

On the CD-ROM
- Grammar Workshop Practice: Using Hyphens Correctly in Compound Words
- Grammar Workshop Test: Using Hyphens Correctly in Compound Words
- Handbook Practice: Hyphens and Dashes

In the Handbook
- Hyphens: 361–362

Additional Resources From Globe Fearon:
- *Globe Exercise Books* Punctuation: 28–29
- *Success in Writing* Grammar Skills for Writers: 80
- *Writer's Toolkit* Handbook: Grammar Handbook: Punctuation: Apostrophes and Hyphens

Writing Manuals

Student Edition, pages 273–276

LEARNING OBJECTIVE

▶ Students will learn how to write a manual.

Lesson Resource

On the *CD-ROM*

• Topic at-a-Glance: Writing Manuals

INTO

Using Prior Knowledge

Bring to class a manual for an appliance or a car. Read the table of contents. What is the purpose of manuals? What problems might a person encounter without manuals? Encourage students to relate their own experiences using manuals. What did students find helpful? confusing? Ask students to preview the lesson headings and captions and predict what they will learn about writing manuals.

THROUGH

Developing the Lesson

This lesson explains what a manual is and how to plan and write one. Students learn that manuals contain an introduction to the product, instructions for setting it up, instructions for using it, technical background about it, and cautionary and reference information about it. The lesson also takes students through the parts of a manual: the covers, the title page, the table of contents, the body, and the index.

Discussing Visuals Review Figure 12-10, *Writing in the Real World: Manual*, on page 275 of the Student Edition. Discuss the callouts. Why is this format suitable for the information it is presenting? Why is each section of the manual important?

BEYOND

Closing the Lesson

Ask groups to make the revisions they suggested in the *Apply What You Learn* activity by rewriting the sections of the manual that required improvement. Ask groups to exchange manuals with one another and critique the old version and the new version. Do the improvements make the manual clearer?

ESL/LEP Tip

Explain that students can understand the meaning of the entire section of a manual by scanning it and then breaking down long explanations into workable sections that they can then make clear. Ask students to work with English-proficient students to practice this strategy.

Web Activity

Many companies make manuals for their products available on the Internet. Ask students to think of a product that they use and find out what company manufactures it. Then, ask students to try to find the manual for that product on the company's Web site. How is the electronic version of the manual similar to paper manuals that they have seen? How are they different?

Using Visuals in Technical Writing

Student Edition, pages 277–278

LEARNING OBJECTIVE

❯ Students will learn to improve written presentations with visual aids.

INTO

Using Prior Knowledge

Ask students if they have ever had to assemble an item. Did the assembly directions include a visual? How did the visual help? Ask students to preview the lesson headings and captions and predict what they will learn about using visuals in technical writing.

THROUGH

Developing the Lesson

Students learn the importance of using visuals to illustrate their writing. They learn that they can use visuals to show objects, compare quantities, illustrate concepts or ideas, and highlight words. They learn that photographs, diagrams, and tables are types of visuals. The lesson also teaches students about formatting visuals, and it provides them with a checklist to use when they include visuals in their writing.

Discussing Visuals Review Figure 12-12 on page 278 of the Student Edition. What does an illustration do that words are not always able to do?

BEYOND

Closing the Lesson

Ask students to critique the one-page technical documents from the *Apply What You Learn* activity as their classmates present them to the class. Do the visuals help to explain the activity? Would the visuals help a person easily recreate the activity?

Extending the Lesson

Ask students to analyze the visuals that technical writers have included in the manuals that you brought to class. Tell students to use the checklist on page 278 of the Student Edition to assess the visuals. Do the visuals help the reader understand what is being said? Are they appropriate to the audience, topic, and purpose? What other kind of visual might have been more effective?

Curriculum Connection: Math

Ask students to examine the graphs in *USA Today*. What kinds of information do these graphs present? Why are these graphs important? How do these visuals make the articles easier to understand?

TECH CONNECTIONS

Use Mail Merge
(Student Edition, page 225)

Ask students to suppose that they were asked to send a mailing to 50 people. How would they approach writing 50 letters and addressing 50 envelopes? Tell students that a mail merge allows them to create a form letter that can be personalized for as many people as necessary. Ask students to work in groups to practice using a mail merge program. Ask each group to draft a form letter to the class. Then, ask each group to compile the names and addresses of the class members into a list and to use the list to personalize its form letter.

Graphic Elements
(Student Edition, page 251)

Tell students that they can use basic word-processing programs to add graphic elements to their documents. Ask them to search for these elements in their computer programs by looking under the Font menu. Then, ask students to share what they have found. What kinds of modifications does their program allow them to make to the text? Does it allow them to change the font type? The point size? Tell students that they should also look at the Symbol command under the Insert menu. What kinds of symbols did they find? Explain to students that they can use symbols—such as checkmarks to design a checklist—in their papers. Ask students whether or not their computers have clip-art.

Format a Technical Document
(Student Edition, page 279)

Ask students to write a one-page document in which they use bullets, centered text, columns, line spacing, margins, numbering, page setup, and tabs. Then, ask students to label each of these on the printed document they create. Ask them to explain how each of these can be important to the overall presentation of a report. Why might it be important to use bullets? to center text? to number pages?

Additional Resource
From Globe Fearon:

*Survival Guide for
Computer Literacy*
Bells and Whistles: 60

UNIT 6

SPEECHES AND PRESENTATIONS

Student Edition, page 283

CAREER FILE PROJECT SUPPORT
On page 330 of the Student Edition, students will read about dental assistants and teachers' aides. Explain that dental assistants work with patients and are responsible for various administrative duties. Becoming a dental assistant would be appropriate for students who are interested in medicine or dentistry. Teachers aides help prepare lesson materials. They also help students with their school-work. Becoming a teachers aide would be ideal for someone who is good at explaining how to do things and enjoys helping children succeed in school.

Action Profile
Ask students to choose one of the two careers profiled in this unit and answer the following questions:

1. What experience, education, and training do employers expect of those they hire?

2. Are there any local or state requirements for working in this field?

3. What interests and traits do students have that would make this a good job for them?

4. Does the job have any requirements students might have difficulty meeting?

5. What related fields might interest students?

As informal talks or formal presentations, speeches are common in business. However, many people are uncomfortable speaking in front of others. The best way to overcome this fear is to feel confident about the material being presented and to have enough practice speaking so that the prospect becomes less frightening. The following lessons offer strategies to help your students gain and practice these skills.

What's in the Unit

This unit begins with Chapter 13, which is about writing and delivering speeches. Students learn how to select and narrow a topic, define the purpose of a speech, write and deliver a speech, and actively listen to other speakers. Chapter 14 focuses on presentations. The chapter discusses how to use visual aids, such as flip charts and slides, in a presentation; how to prepare a presentation; how to create handouts for and give a presentation; and how to be an effective participant at a meeting.

Previewing the Unit

Ask students what they think a speech is. Then, ask them to preview the unit by looking at the titles, headings, subheadings, figures, photos, illustrations, captions and key words. Ask students what they think the main points of these chapters will be. Then, ask students how being able to prepare and give a speech will be useful at school and at work. What other kinds of situations does learning to give a speech prepare students for?

Developing the Unit

Ask students to imagine that they are working in a job that interests them. What speeches and presentations might they have to listen to? What kinds of speeches might they have to deliver? Explain to students that the ability to deliver and listen to speeches is a skill they will use often in their jobs.

ACTIVITY	MINUTES
Preview lesson headings, captions, and boldfaced words; discuss students' experiences with speeches and presentations	10
Read and discuss Lessons 13-1 and 13-2	20
Small groups meet to discuss *Apply What You Learn*, Lesson 13-1	10
Writing: Students work on the Job Path Project by selecting a topic and narrowing it for their speech	20
Discuss Grammar Workshop: Working with Prepositions	15
Small groups meet to discuss *Apply What You Learn*, Lesson 13-2	10
Concluding reflections, assignments, and answer questions	5

IN-DEPTH DISCOVERY

Resources for students to explore include

- *Say It With Confidence: Overcoming the Mental Blocks That Keep You from Making Great Presentations & Speeches* by Margo T. Krasne. New York: Warner Books, 1997. This book explains how nervous speakers can overcome shyness and panic attacks while learning how to behave dynamically.

- *101 Secrets of Highly Effective Speakers: Controlling Fear, Commanding Attention* by Caryl Rae Krannich. San Luis Obispo, CA: Impact Publications, 1998. This book offers practical ideas that will help develop the skills and confidence necessary to present a successful speech.

- *7 Steps to Fearless Speaking* by Lilyan Wilder. New York: John Wiley & Sons, 1999. This book explains how to structure a presentation, use props, and demonstrate conviction.

Within the Family

Students can ask family members about speeches they have presented and listened to at work. What makes a speech effective? What makes a speech less effective? Ask students to take notes on what the adults tell them about speeches. Then, ask students to write a one-page summary about what they learned.

Job Path Project

Students will deliver a speech to their classmates about their career choice. They will select and narrow a topic, define the purpose of their speech, and write and deliver their final presentation.

Discussing the Quote

Ask students to read the quote by Ralph Waldo Emerson on page 283 of the Student Edition. How does this quote relate to speeches and presentations? What might Ralph Waldo Emerson say about a speech as a tool for persuasion?

Closing the Unit

Assess students' understanding of this unit by writing the vocabulary words on the chalkboard and asking the students for definitions. Then, discuss occasions when students might present a speech. Ask students to imagine that they have been chosen to give a speech. What steps would they take to create an effective speech? As your students complete each chapter in this unit, you can use the chapter assessments located on the CD-ROM to check their progress.

Student Edition, pages 284–285

WRITING AND DELIVERING A SPEECH
English in Context

TEACHING THE CHAPTER OPENER

Emma works as a dental assistant and has been asked to address a group of high school students about her job. Emma is excited by the opportunity but is apprehensive because she does not know how to prepare or present a speech. Many people feel the way Emma does about giving a speech, even though public speaking is more common than most students realize. In this chapter, students will study how to write a speech, how to give it with confidence, and how to listen to and learn from other speakers.

• Ask students to brainstorm times when employees might give speeches. Why is giving an effective speech important?

PORTFOLIO SETUP: WRITING AND DELIVERING A SPEECH

• On page 305 of the Student Edition, students are asked to write and present a speech. You can combine this project with the Job Path Project and ask students to write their speeches about the career they are interested in. Possible topics include a day in the life of a person in that field, an examination of possible careers in that field, or a recent discovery or advancement in that field. Ask students to begin thinking about this project at the beginning of Chapter 13 and to develop it as they complete each lesson.

CD-ROM TEAMWORK/COOPERATIVE ACTIVITY

• Students work in groups to create a "state of the school" address. Each student in the group chooses to take on the role of the researcher, who investigates the topic; the speechwriter, who drafts and edits the speech; or the speaker, who presents it to the class or school.

LESSON PLANNING CHART			
CHAPTER 13	**STUDENT EDITION PAGES**	**TEACHER'S RESOURCE MANUAL PAGES**	**CD-ROM**
Writing/Reading Activities	288, 295, 301–305	119, 122–126	✓
Speaking/Listening Activities	294, 299, 301, 304, 305	119, 124, 125	✓
Career Activities	305	120, 122	✓
Critical Thinking Activities	286, 288–291, 294, 296, 299–301, 304, 305	119–122, 124, 125	✓
Vocabulary Activities	285, 304	121	✓
ESL/LEP Tips		120, 121, 125	
Teamwork/Cooperative Activities	294, 299, 304	119, 124, 125	✓
Curriculum Connections		121	
Technology Activities	303	122, 135	

Selecting a Topic
Student Edition, pages 286–288

LEARNING OBJECTIVE

▶ Students will learn how to select a topic or message for a speech.

Lesson Resource

On the *CD-ROM*

• Topic at-a-Glance: Selecting a Topic

INTO
Using Prior Knowledge
Ask students to talk about memorable speeches they have heard. How does listening to a speech differ from reading the same information? Ask students to preview the lesson headings and captions and predict what they will learn about selecting a topic.

THROUGH
Developing the Lesson
Students learn how to select a topic and prepare a speech by thinking about the audience, the other speakers' topics, the length of the speech, and the occasion at which it is being presented. Then, they learn to narrow a topic by using an example, shortening the time period, focusing on a part of the whole, limiting by purpose, doing more research and brainstorming, and writing the topic in one sentence.

Discussing Visuals Review Figures 13-1, 13-2, 13-3, and 13-4 on pages 287 and 288 of the Student Edition. Ask students what they should consider when narrowing a topic. How can the approaches in Figures 13-1 through 13-4 be useful when narrowing a topic?

BEYOND
Closing the Lesson
After students complete the *Apply What You Learn* activity, ask them to refer to the four different ways their topics can be narrowed and to decide which is the most effective. Is using an example the best way? shortening the time period? focusing on a part of the whole? How do their topics affect the way they choose to narrow them? Ask students to explain their answers.

ESL/LEP Tip
Ask the class to brainstorm broad topics. Write the students' suggestions on the chalkboard. Then, ask students to work with English-proficient students to practice using the methods presented on pages 287 and 288 of the Student Edition to narrow three of the topics.

Job Path Project
Ask students to take the first step toward preparing a speech about the career they chose by choosing and narrowing a topic. What facet of their field do they want to share with the class? What method should they use to narrow their topic? Remind students to think about the audience they will be addressing. What information would their classmates find interesting?

Additional Resources
From Globe Fearon:

• *Globe Exercise Books*
  Paragraphs: 10–11

• *Success in Writing*
  Writing to Describe: 19–23, 40, 50
  Writing to Explain: 9, 20–24, 48–49
  Writing to Persuade: 20–24

• *Writer's Toolkit*
  Choosing a Topic: Issues Wheel Research Paper Topic Bin; Narrowing a Topic: Topic Web, Cluster Diagram Considering Audience and Purpose: Audience Profile

Defining the Purpose of the Speech

Student Edition, pages 289–290

LEARNING OBJECTIVE

▶ Students will learn how to define the purpose of a speech.

Lesson Resources

On the *CD-ROM*

- Topic at-a-Glance: Defining the Purpose of the Speech
- Application: Defining the Purpose of the Speech

Additional Resources From Globe Fearon:

- *Globe Exercise Books*
  Paragraphs: 16–19

- *Success in Writing*
  Writing to Describe: 24, 27, 43–44, 63–64, 70
  Writing to Explain: 10, 24, 25, 57
  Writing to Persuade: 25, 27

- *Writer's Toolkit*
  Considering Audience and Purpose: Purpose Profile; Organizing Details: Timeline

INTO

Using Prior Knowledge

Write *persuade, inform,* and *entertain* on the chalkboard. Ask students to think about speeches that might fall into these categories. What made the speech persuasive? informative? entertaining? Write students' answers on the board. Ask students to preview the lesson headings and captions and predict what they will learn.

THROUGH

Developing the Lesson

Students learn that the purpose of a speech is to persuade, inform, entertain, or a combination of any of these. Students learn that a persuasive speech tries to move listeners to action, an informative speech instructs and explains, and an entertaining speech is designed to amuse.

Discussing Visuals Review Figure 13-5 on page 290 of the Student Edition. Discuss with students the different types of purposes and the example openers for each of them. Which characteristics distinguish a persuasive opener from an informative opener? from an entertaining opener?

BEYOND

Closing the Lesson

Ask students to refer to the topics they brainstormed for the *Apply What You Learn* activity. Then, ask them to write a persuasive opener, an informative opener, and an entertaining opener for their topics. How do each of these differ?

Curriculum Connection: History

Ask students to identify a famous speech. Some possible speeches include Abraham Lincoln's "Gettysburg Address," or Franklin Delano Roosevelt's "Four Freedoms" speech or his weekly radio addresses. What is the purpose of the speech each student chose? How is the speech persuasive, informative, or entertaining?

ESL/LEP Tip

Ask students to work with English-proficient students to define the terms *persuasive, informative,* and *entertaining.* Ask English-proficient students to review the example openers on page 290 of the Student Edition with students to understand what makes the first opener persuasive, the second informative, and the third entertaining.

LESSON 13-3

Writing the Speech
Student Edition, pages 291–294

LEARNING OBJECTIVE

▶ Students will learn how to write a speech.

Lesson Resources

On the *CD-ROM*

• Topic at-a-Glance: Writing the Speech

• Application: Writing the Speech

Additional Resources
From Globe Fearon:

• *Globe Exercise Books*
  Paragraphs: 8–9, 32–33

• *Success in Writing*
  Writing to Describe: 29–31
  Writing to Explain: 25, 29–32, 70
  Writing to Persuade: 26, 30–32

• *Writer's Toolkit*
  Writing Tools: Organizing Details: Outline; The Writing Process: Drafting; Writing Handbook: Revising and Editing; Elements of Nonfiction: Using Resources

• *Reading in the Content Areas*
  Level A: 8–11
  Level D: 8–11

• *Be a Better Reader*
  Level B: 140–141
  Level C: 92–93
  Level E: 92–93
  Level F: 112–113

INTO
Using Prior Knowledge
Discuss what makes a speech effective. How does the language contribute to a speaker's message? How does a good speaker get an audience's attention? Ask students to preview the lesson headings and captions and predict what they will learn about writing speeches.

THROUGH
Developing the Lesson
Students learn how to write a speech. They learn to gather material through firsthand experience, others' experiences, and traditional research. Then, they learn to organize the information using chronological, or time, order; topical order; problem-solution order; or a combination of these methods. Students learn to construct an outline; write a speech; include an introduction, a body, and a conclusion in their speech; and edit their final work.

Discussing Visuals Review Figure 13-7, *Writing in the Real World: A Speech*, on page 293 of the Student Edition. Discuss the callouts. How does the speech keep its audience's attention?

BEYOND
Closing the Lesson
Ask students to complete the *Apply What You Learn* activity. Ask students to give three reasons why they believe the speech was organized the way they think it was organized.

Web Activity
There are many sites on the Web that offer tips for writing and giving speeches, including the following:
www.learn2.com/06/0694/0694.php3
www.la.psu.edu/speech/100a/workbook/wrkbk.html
www.studyweb.com/links/2368.html

Job Path Project
Ask students to continue working on their Job Path Projects by gathering and organizing material. Ask students to decide which order would most effectively fit their speech and to construct an outline. Then, ask students to write their speeches, and remind them to include an introduction, a body, and a conclusion. Tell students to refer to pages 292 and 294 of the Student Edition to refresh their understanding of the parts of a speech. Explain to students that they can use Figure 13-7 on page 293 of the Student Edition as a model for their speeches.

Grammar Workshop

TIP

Tell students that when they are trying to decide on subject–verb agreement, they should always ignore the intervening prepositional phrases. For example, *That group [of employees] is in charge of Human Resources.*

Lesson Resources

On the *CD-ROM*

- Grammar Workshop Practice: Working With Prepositions
- Grammar Workshop Test: Working With Prepositions
- Handbook Practice: Prepositions

In the *Handbook*

- Prepositions: 356

Additional Resources From Globe Fearon:

- *Globe Exercise Books* Parts of Speech: 36–39
- *Success in Writing* Grammar Skills for Writers: 38–39

WORKING WITH PREPOSITIONS

Grammar Workshop at-a-Glance

This Grammar Workshop focuses on prepositions, which show the location, direction, or time relationships between a noun or pronoun and other words in a sentence.

Error Alert: Solving the Problem

- Write this sentence on the chalkboard: *Lynn keeps her cup on her desk.*

- Ask students, *What is the prepositional phrase in this sentence?* (on her desk)

- Write this sentence on the board: *The delivery van drove past our building several times.*

- Ask students, *What is the prepositional phrase in this sentence?* (past our building)

- Write this sentence on the board: *Cleo finished before lunch.*

- Ask students, *What is the prepositional phrase in this sentence?* (before lunch)

- Write this sentence on the chalkboard: *The new office comes with a kitchen.*

- Ask students, *What is the prepositional phrase in this sentence?* (with a kitchen)

- Write this sentence on the chalkboard: *Tarek works across the hall from Elysa.*

- Ask students, *What are the two prepositional phrases in this sentence?* (across the hall, from Elysa)

✎ Write the following sentences on the board. Ask students to identify the prepositional phrase in each sentence.

1. He restocked the supply room until quitting time. (until quitting time)

2. For lunch, I had a sandwich. (For lunch)

3. The office manager records appointments on her computer. (on her computer)

4. Greta is among the two remaining candidates. (among the two remaining candidates)

5. She asked him to wait inside the lobby. (inside the lobby)

Delivering the Speech

Student Edition, pages 296–299

LEARNING OBJECTIVE

▶ Students will learn how to present a speech to persuade, inform, or entertain.

Lesson Resources

🖸 **On the *CD-ROM***

• Topic at-a-Glance: Delivering the Speech

• Application: Checklist for Delivering the Speech

• Application: Delivering the Speech

• Teamwork/Cooperative Activity: Delivering the Speech

Additional Resources
From Globe Fearon:

• *Globe Exercise Books*
Paragraphs: 8–9

• *Writer's Toolkit*
Writing Tools: Organizing Details: Outliner

• *Reading in the Content Areas*
Level A: 8–11
Level D: 8–11

• *Be a Better Reader*
Level B: 140–141
Level C: 92–93
Level E: 92–93
Level F: 112–113

INTO

Using Prior Knowledge

Ask students to discuss how they felt when they had to give a speech and were not adequately prepared. Were they nervous? Then, ask them what happened when they prepared their speeches in advance. Did they feel more self-confident? How did they prepare their notes for the speech? Then, ask students to preview the lesson headings and captions and predict what they will learn about delivering a speech.

THROUGH

Developing the Lesson

This lesson describes how to prepare notes for and deliver a speech. Students learn that note cards, an outline, and a manuscript are three ways to prepare notes. They learn that it is important to practice their speeches and focus on gestures and posture, vocal techniques, eye contact, and facial expressions. Finally, the lesson offers advice on presenting the speech and dealing with interruptions. Review the checklist on pages 298 and 299 of the Student Edition. How is each point important when giving a speech?

BEYOND

Closing the Lesson

Ask students to refer to the speech they watched on television for the *Apply What You Learn* activity. Ask students to analyze the speech by evaluating the speaker's delivery. What kinds of gestures did the speaker use? Ask students to describe the speaker's body language and posture. Did the speaker use a monotone? use his or her voice to emphasize main points? Did the speaker speak slowly and clearly? Did he or she make eye contact or use facial expressions?

Job Path Project

Divide the class into small groups. To reinforce the importance of practicing before your peers, ask students to practice presenting the speeches they wrote for the Job Path Project. Ask students to critique their classmates' speeches. Ask students to describe their classmates' body language and posture. Did they use a monotone, or did they use their voices to emphasize main points? Did they speak slowly and clearly? Did they make eye contact with the members of the group, and did they use facial expressions to communicate their message?

LEARNING OBJECTIVE

▶ Students will learn to actively listen to the speeches given by others

Active Listening

Student Edition, pages 300–301

INTO

Using Prior Knowledge

Ask students to think about situations in which they get their information by listening. What are some of these situations? How do they make sure that they are hearing everything that is being said? Ask students to preview the lesson headings and captions and predict what they will learn about active listening.

THROUGH

Developing the Lesson

This lesson focuses on active listening. Students learn the difference between active and passive listening. They learn how to listen actively by paying attention, keeping an open mind, and thinking about what they already know. They learn that responsive listening, critical listening, and informational listening are all types of active listening. Ask students to take notes while you discuss the lesson. When you finish the lesson, ask students to close their books and summarize the main points that they have learned. How many students were actively listening?

BEYOND

Closing the Lesson

Ask students to work in groups and compare the notes and summaries they wrote for the *Apply What You Learn* activity. What is the best way to listen to the speech that students analyzed? If students had an approach that was different from the members of their group, ask students to explain their choices. Ask group members to actively listen to their classmates' explanations. Were their explanations convincing?

Extending the Lesson

An important part of listening actively is knowing how to take notes. Ask students to suppose that they work for a radio station. Tell them to work in groups and decide on a topic about which they would like to prepare a newscast. Ask students to narrow their topic, consider their audience, script their newscast, and deliver it to the class. Ask the class to actively listen to the newscast and take notes. Then ask students to refer to their notes and summarize the information they listened to. What techniques did they use to record the information they heard? Did they note main ideas? details?

ESL/LEP Tip

Students may have difficulty understanding speeches. Ask students to listen to television or radio news programs and write a brief summary of a news report.

Grammar Workshop

TIP

Explain to students that a colon introduces what is to follow; a semicolon separates grammatically similar forms.

Lesson Resources

On the *CD-ROM*

• Grammar Workshop Practice: Using Colons Correctly

• Grammar Workshop Test: Using Colons Correctly

• Handbook Practice: Semicolons and Colons

In the *Handbook*

• Colons: 360

USING COLONS CORRECTLY

Grammar Workshop at-a-Glance

This Grammar Workshop explains how to use colons after the greeting in a business letter, between the hour and minutes when telling time, when an independent clause introduces a list, and when introducing a sentence, question, or formal quotation.

Error Alert: Solving the Problem

• Write this phrase on the chalkboard: *To the Office of the President*

• Tell students, *This is a greeting.* Ask students, *Is this correct?* (No; it needs a colon after *President.*)

• Write this sentence on the chalkboard: *The company cafeteria is open for lunch from 1100 to 230.*

• Ask students, *Is this correct?* (No; *1100* should be *11:00* and *230* should be *2:30.*)

• Write this sentence on the chalkboard: *The project team consisted of three people the researcher, the writer, and the designer.*

• Ask students, *Is this correct?* (No; it needs a colon after *people.*)

• Write this sentence on the chalkboard: *In one passage of his famous pamphlet, Thomas Paine writes "The cause of America is in great measure the cause of all mankind."*

• Ask students, *Is this correct?* (No; it needs a colon after *writes*.)

🖉 Write the following sentences on the board. Ask students to rewrite the following items by inserting colons where needed.

1. To the Customer Service Department at Services, Inc. (Inc.:)

2. The chef uses three basic spices in his cooking oregano, basil, and rosemary. (cooking:)

3. Martin Luther King, Jr., said "If I am stopped, this movement will not stop, for what we are doing is right." (said:)

4. Dr. Percy sees patients from 900 A.M. to 600 P.M. (9:00, 6:00)

5. In an interview with a writer, President Woodrow Wilson exclaimed "Liberty is always attained by the forces working below, underneath, by the great movement of the people." (exclaimed:)

Additional Resources From Globe Fearon:

• *Globe Exercise Books*
Punctuation: 24–25

• *Success in Writing*
Grammar Skills for Writers: 73

Student Edition, pages 306–307

WRITING AND GIVING PRESENTATIONS

English in Context

TEACHING THE CHAPTER OPENER

Jodi has a chance to work part-time for a summer camp giving presentations at local high schools to recruit employees. The job sounds like fun, but Jodi does not know much about giving a presentation. She knows that being able to confidently deliver a presentation will make her a more valuable employee. In this chapter, students will learn how to prepare and deliver a presentation.

• Ask students to discuss sales presentations, school presentations, or presentations on television that they have seen. What skills would students need to create and deliver a presentation?

PORTFOLIO SETUP: WRITING A PRESENTATION

• On page 329, students are asked to plan and prepare a presentation. Ask students to choose a topic that they would like to spend time developing. It might be connected to a career or to an extracurricular activity that interests them. Ask students to begin thinking about a subject for their presentation. Then, tell them to develop their presentation as the chapter progresses.

CD-ROM TEAMWORK/COOPERATIVE ACTIVITY

• This activity asks students to work with a group of classmates to prepare a presentation about the best summer jobs available for teenagers. Each student in the group chooses to take on a certain role such as that of a researcher, who investigates the topic; a writer, who uses the research to write the presentation; a graphic artist, who creates the visuals for the presentation; a technician, who arranges to make any necessary equipment available; or a speaker, who delivers the presentation.

LESSON PLANNING CHART			
CHAPTER 14	STUDENT EDITION PAGES	TEACHER'S RESOURCE MANUAL PAGES	CD-ROM
Writing/Reading Activities	310, 314, 315, 318, 321, 322, 326, 328–330	127, 129–134	✓
Speaking/Listening Activities	310, 314, 321, 329	127–129, 131, 132, 134	✓
Career Activities	326, 329, 330	129, 132	✓
Critical Thinking Activities	308, 311, 316, 318, 319, 321, 323, 326	127, 128, 131, 132, 134	✓
Vocabulary Activities	307, 328		✓
ESL/LEP Tips		128, 131	
Teamwork/Cooperative Activities	310, 314, 321	127, 131, 132	✓
Curriculum Connections		128, 132	
Technology Activities	310, 327	129, 134, 135	✓

Using Visuals Aids in a Presentation

Student Edition, pages 308–310

LEARNING OBJECTIVE

▶ Students will learn how to organize material for a presentation.

INTO

Using Prior Knowledge

Ask students if they have ever seen a presentation that used slides or transparencies. What did these visuals add to the presentation? Did they make the presentation easier to understand? Then, ask students to preview the lesson headings and captions and predict what they will learn about using visual aids in a presentation.

THROUGH

Developing the Lesson

Students learn that flip charts, transparencies, slides, and videos are types of visual aids. They also learn about the importance of visuals and how to choose and prepare them for a presentation. Review the checklist for creating effective text-based slides or transparencies on pages 309 and 310 of the Student Edition. How can a word-processing program create visuals?

BEYOND

Closing the Lesson

Ask the class to critique each group's presentation from the *Apply What You Learn* activity. Which visual aids did each group choose? Did the visual aids effectively communicate key points? Which visual aids were most effective? Which visual aids require improvement? Ask students to brainstorm ways to make the visual aids that require improvement more effective.

Discussing Visuals Review figure 14-1 on page 309 of the Student Edition. What makes one of these slides easier to read than the other?

ESL/LEP Tip

The visuals that are used in presentations can be invaluable to students because they show the same information the students hear. Explain that some of the most important points of a presentation are often included on visuals. Tell students that paying close attention to visuals can help them understand the information in presentations. As students give their presentations, help students identify the importance of each visual aid that is used.

Curriculum Connection: Social Studies

Ask students to think about the visual aids that their social studies teachers have used. How did these visual aids help students understand the information? Why would the teachers use charts, graphs, and diagrams for social studies presentations?

Preparing Your Presentation

Student Edition, pages 311–314

LEARNING OBJECTIVE

▶ Students will learn how to prepare a presentation.

Lesson Resource

🖥 **On the *CD-ROM***

• Topic at-a-Glance: Preparing Your Presentation

Additional Resources From Globe Fearon:

• *Globe Exercise Books*
  Paragraphs: 8–9

• *Success in Writing*
  Writing to Describe: 29–31
  Writing to Explain: 8, 25, 29–32, 70
  Writing to Persuade: 26, 30–32

• *Writer's Toolkit*
  Writing Tools: Organizing
  Details: Outliner

• *Reading in the Content Areas*
  Level A: 8–11
  Level D: 8–11

• *Be a Better Reader*
  Level B: 140–141
  Level C: 92–93
  Level E: 92–93
  Level F: 112–113

INTO

Using Prior Knowledge

What do students do when they have to organize something? Ask students to discuss the strategies they use to organize research information, their writing, and visual aids. Ask students to preview the lesson headings and captions and predict what they will learn about preparing a presentation.

THROUGH

Developing the Lesson

Students learn the first steps in organizing a presentation. Then, students learn how to write a thesis statement and an outline. Students also learn that the introduction, body, and conclusion are the three parts of a presentation. Finally, students learn how to organize the visuals in their presentations by using a storyboard.

Discussing Visuals Review Figure 14-2, *Writing in the Real World: Presentation Note Cards*, on page 313 of the Student Edition. Why are note cards useful during a presentation?

BEYOND

Closing the Lesson

Ask students to prepare presentation note cards for the outline they wrote in the *Apply What You Learn* activity. Ask students to deliver their presentation to their partners. Do the presentation note cards include all the information that the speaker will need during the presentation?

Job Path Project

Ask students to create a presentation by adding visual aids to the speech they wrote about their career of choice in Chapter 13. Encourage students to develop a storyboard to organize their visuals. Then, ask students to create presentation note cards that highlight key points and cue important visuals in their presentation.

Web Activity

Refer students to the following Web sites for more information on making effective presentations:

sol.brunel.ac.uk/~jarvis/study/skills12.html

www.bcs.org.uk/ypg/jobhunt/making.htm

www.cba.neu.edu/~ewertheim/skills/oral.htm

Grammar Workshop

Student Edition, page 315

Lesson Resources

On the *CD-Rom*

- Grammar Workshop Practice: Forming Irregular Plurals
- Grammar Workshop Test: Forming Irregular Plurals
- Handbook Practice: Singular, Plural, and Collective Nouns

In the *Handbook*

- Nouns: 349

Additional Resources From Globe Fearon:

- *Globe Exercise Books*
  Spelling and Vocabulary: 6–7

- *Success in Writing*
  Grammar Skills for Writers: 113–114

FORMING IRREGULAR PLURALS

Grammar Workshop at-a-Glance

This Grammar Workshop teaches students some basic rules about forming irregular plurals. Students learn that nouns ending in *-s*, *-ch*, *-z*, *-sh*, or *–x*, add *-es* to form their plurals and that nouns ending in *–y* drop the *-y* and add *–ies*. Students also learn that some nouns are irregular and follow no pattern.

Error Alert: Solving the Problem

- Write this sentence on the board: *How many company are participating in this year's seminar?*

- Ask students, *Is this correct?* (No; *company* should be *companies*.)

- Write this sentence on the board: *Our company participated in Bring Your Childs to Work Week.*

- Ask students, *Is this correct?* (No; *Childs* should be *Children*.)

- Write this sentence on the board: *Two man and two woman share the medical practice.*

- Ask students, *Is this correct?* (No; *man* should be *men* and *woman* should be *women*.)

- Write this sentence on the chalkboard: *Chef Charles used one of his professional knifes to cut the two cake.*

- Ask students, *Is this correct?* (No; *knifes* should be *knives* and *cake* should be *cakes*.)

Write the following sentences on the chalkboard. Ask students to rewrite each sentence using the correct plural form of the underlined noun.

1. All employees were asked to bring their <u>husband</u> and <u>wife</u> to the company holiday party. (husbands, wives)

2. TechLand hired five new computer <u>expert</u>. (experts)

3. Marjorie scanned two <u>bagfull</u> of vegetable for her customer. (bagsfull, vegetables)

4. Pelson Place, Inc., occupies 400 square <u>foot</u> of office space. (feet)

5. The pastry chef cuts the fruit into <u>half</u>, and then uses the two pieces to make pies for all three <u>party</u>. (halves, parties)

Creating Handouts for a Presentation

Student Edition, pages 316–318

INTO

Using Prior Knowledge

Bring samples of handouts to class so that students can see what they look like. Ask students if they know what handouts are and what purpose they might have. How might handouts be useful? Ask students to preview the lesson headings and captions and predict what they will learn.

THROUGH

Developing the Lesson

This lesson teaches students the purposes of handouts. Students learn that handouts can inform, persuade, and entertain. Then, students learn how to prepare a handout that informs, a handout that persuades, and a handout that entertains.

Discussing Visuals Review Figure 14-3 on page 317 of the Student Edition. Ask students to determine the different purposes of each of the handouts in Figure 14-3. How can they tell when a handout is meant to inform? persuade? entertain? Review Figures 14-4 and 14-5 on page 318 of the Student Edition. What is the purpose of each of these handouts? Are they successful? How can they be improved?

BEYOND

Closing the Lesson

Ask students to exchange with a classmate the one-page handouts that they wrote for the *Apply What You Learn* activity. Ask students to critique the handout. Is it effective? How can it be improved?

ESL/LEP Tip

Explain to students that some handouts are designed to include the main points of a presentation. Tell them that there are two ways that these handouts can be a valuable resource for understanding a presentation. Tell students that they can preview a handout before a presentation to see what the speaker will cover and think about what they know about the subject. They can also use the handouts as a basis for taking notes. As the speaker delivers his or her main points, students can write their notes under each point listed on the handouts. Tell students to practice using these strategies the next time they are given handouts in class or on the job. Once students have had a chance to try the strategies, ask them to summarize how these strategies helped them. Why was it useful having the main points of the presentation ahead of time?

Giving a Presentation
Student Edition, pages 319–321

LEARNING OBJECTIVE

▶ Students will learn how to give a presentation.

Lesson Resources

On the *CD-ROM*

- Application: Giving a Presentation
- Application: Checklist for Giving a Presentation
- Teamwork/Cooperative Activity: Giving a Presentation

INTO

Using Prior Knowledge

Ask students to think of a presentation they have heard. Encourage them to discuss what makes a presentation successful. What are some approaches and techniques a speaker should avoid? Ask students to preview the lesson headings and captions and predict what they will learn.

THROUGH

Developing the Lesson

This lesson describes how to prepare a presentation and suggests adding sound to enhance it. Students learn that presenters should arrive early, set up and test their equipment, and make any last-minute adjustments to their presentations. Then, students learn how to handle visual aids and sound during a presentation and how to conduct a question-and-answer period at the end of a presentation. Review the checklist for handling visual aids and sound on page 321 of the Student Edition. Why is it important to set up and test the equipment *before* a presentation? Review the tips on how to conduct a question-and-answer period at the end of the presentation. How does each of these tips make a question-and-answer period successful and informative?

BEYOND

Closing the Lesson

Ask students in each group to use the guidelines they created for the *Apply What You Learn* activity to analyze a television newscast. One student can concentrate on the news, another on the sports, and another on the weather. How effective was each presentation? How could each one be improved?

Curriculum Connection: Social Studies

Ask students to think about a presentation they have heard that used audio and visual aids. Then, ask students to explain how audio and visual aids helped the speaker communicate his or her point more effectively. What kinds of audio and visual aids did the speaker use? How did they help the speaker communicate his or her point?

Job Path Project

Ask students to add audio aids to the presentations they have been working on. Tell students to review what they should do before, during, and after a presentation as shown on pages 319–321 of the Student Edition. Then, ask students to deliver their presentations.

TIP

Explain to students that proof-reading marks can be used to revise any type of writing they do. They can be used to correct a résumé, a research paper, or a presentation.

Lesson Resources

On the *CD-ROM*

- Grammar Workshop Practice: Using Proofreading Marks
- Grammar Workshop Test: Using Proofreading Marks

In the *Handbook*

- Proofreading Checklist: 343

USING PROOFREADING MARKS

Grammar Workshop at-a-Glance

This Grammar Workshop discusses proofreading marks. Students learn that proofreading marks are shorthand that they can use to identify areas that need to be revised.

Here are the most commonly used proofreader's marks:

delete	⟋	insert	∧
no space	͡	add space	the photos
add period	⊙	add comma	∧
add apostrophe	∨	add quotation marks	∨ ∨
move text	prices sale	new paragraph	¶
lowercase	✗	capitalize	≡

✎ Write this paragraph on the chalkboard and ask students to revise it using proofreading marks:

Lately our office has considered going on line. To do our banking. We knows several companie that do already all there transactions' on line, and they praise the feature's of online banking. suchas being able for check and look at accounts iafter banking hours. I knows that if it were done by us, we would first need to convince, the boss Mr mcGruder

Corrected Version

Lately‸our office has considered going on‿line. To do our banking. We knows several companie‸that do already all the‸re transactions on‿line, and they praise the feature's of online banking. suchas being able‸for check and look at accounts iafter banking hours. I knows that if‸it were done by us, we would first need to convince the boss‸Mr.mcGruder.

Additional Resource
From Globe Fearon:

- *Success in Writing*
  Grammar Skills for Writers: 107

Attending Meetings

Student Edition, pages 323–326

LEARNING OBJECTIVES

▶ Students will learn how to run a meeting and how to be an active participant.

INTO

Using Prior Knowledge

Ask students to think about a meeting that they have participated in. What made the meeting productive? unproductive? Write students' answers on the chalkboard. Ask students to preview the lesson headings and captions and predict what they will learn about the attending meetings.

THROUGH

Developing the Lesson

Students learn how to prepare for a meeting they are organizing. The lesson also includes tips for running a meeting, such as starting on time and running the meeting skillfully. The lesson explains parliamentary procedure and gives students tips for attending meetings. Finally, this lesson provides a checklist to evaluate how effective a meeting is. Review the steps for preparing for a meeting on pages 323–324 of the Student Edition. How can preparation help to ensure that the characteristics of an effective meeting listed on page 326 of the Student Edition will be met?

Discussing Visuals Review Figure 14-6 on page 324 of the Student Edition. Why is it important to build extra time into an agenda?

BEYOND

Closing the Lesson

Ask students to use the agenda they wrote for the *Apply What You Learn* activity to role-play an actual meeting that might occur in this situation. One or two students can be assistant managers; other students can be members of the restaurant's staff. Encourage students to review the steps for preparing, running, and attending a meeting. After the meeting, ask each group to analyze how effective its meeting was when it used the checklist of characteristics of an effective meeting on page 326 of the Student Edition. What did the group do well? What can it improve? How?

Web Activity

The Internet offers good advice about how to make a meeting effective and successful:

www.infoteam.com/nonprofit/nica/Effmeet.html

www.peopleandplanet.org/og/effect.htm

www.team-creations.com/meeting.htm

www.students.uci.edu/publications/guides/c2.html

TECH CONNECTIONS

Online Research Resources
(Student Edition, page 303)

There is a wealth of useful information available on the Web. However, caution students that some Web sites are more credible than others. Explain to your students the importance of evaluating and validating sources from the Web. Also, tell students that searching online is very different from book-based research. Because Web sites exist in a hyper-linked universe, they can send students far from their intended targets. Tell students that it is important to focus on the topics they chose while conducting their research.

Computer Programs for Presentations
(Student Edition, page 327)

Tell students that computer programs designed to create presentations are easy to use, and the results can be professional looking. These programs offer a template that is ready to use when preparing a presenation. Another option is the AutoContent Wizard that allows the computer to create a series of pages based on user input. Ask students to create a presentation using each of these methods. What are the advantages of each? the disadvantages?

**Additional Resources
From Globe Fearon:**

*Survival Guide for
Computer Literacy:* 60, 100

On the *CD-ROM*
Topic at-a–Glance: Evaluating
Sources
Application: Evaluating Sources

Literature Connections

Here are suggestions for connecting the lessons in each chapter to a literary work. While each of these activities can be used with many different pieces of literature, suggested readings have been included.

CHAPTER 1: Your Career Goals

Ask students to choose a character from their reading and assume a character's identity. As the character, ask students to assess the character's skills, decide which work habits will be helpful, and set career goals.

Suggested Reading:

A Raisin in the Sun	*My Ántonia*
Macbeth	*The Phantom of the Opera*

CHAPTER 2: Finding the Right Job

Ask students to choose a character from their reading and assume the character's identity. Then, ask students to find the right job for that character. What are his or her strengths? weaknesses? likes? dislikes? As the character, ask students to write a résumé and cover letter applying for the job they chose for the character. Then, ask students to work with a partner to role-play an interview. Would the class give this character the job?

Suggested Reading:

Beowulf	*Little Women*
Great Expectations	*O. Henry*

CHAPTER 3: Being Competent in the Workplace

Ask students to choose a problem that the characters faced in the reading they chose. Then, ask students to assume the roles of the characters and design two skits that show the characters making decisions and resolving their conflict.

Suggested Reading:

Julius Caesar	*Romeo and Juliet*
Moby Dick	*Silas Marner*

CHAPTERS 4 & 5: Beginning and Completing the Writing Process

Using the writing process, ask students to create a class newspaper. Each student can perform one of the following tasks: write a lead story that gives the details of one key event from the reading; write a letter to the Editor that gives an opinion of an issue or event from the reading; create pictures that represent characters, places, and conflicts; write an advice column; or create a classified ad section.

Suggested Reading:

A Doll's House	*The Odyssey*
A Tale of Two Cities	*The Red Badge of Courage*

CHAPTER 6: Reading and Writing Directions

Ask students to choose a character from their reading who requires directions to complete a task or to get to a particular location. Ask students to write a set of directions in memo form for the character that helps the character complete the task or arrive at his or her final destination.

Suggested Reading:

Gulliver's Travels	*Lord Jim*
Heart of Darkness	*The Odyssey*

CHAPTER 7: Writing to Explain a Process

Ask students to choose a character from their reading and assume the character's identity. Then, ask students to describe how the character changes. Students can describe this process in the form of a letter or a reflective journal entry. Students should include the reasons why the character changed and the outcome of the character's transformation.

Suggested Reading:

The Call of the Wild	*Jane Eyre*
Frankenstein	*The Jungle*

CHAPTER 8: Writing Reports That Describe

Ask students to choose a character from their reading and assume the character's identity. Then, tell students to describe three other characters from the reading from the perspective of the character they chose. Explain to students that they will need to provide details about each character.

Suggested Reading:

The Canterbury Tales   *Pride and Prejudice*
Great Expectations   *The Scarlet Letter*

CHAPTER 9: Writing To Persuade

Ask students to write a persuasive letter to the character in which they try to convince the character of something.

Suggested Reading:

Ethan Frome   *Romeo and Juliet*
Julius Caesar   *Things Fall Apart*

CHAPTER 10: Writing Business Letters

Ask students to choose a character from their reading and assume the character's identity. What kind of a business could this character have? What might this character's business need? As the character from the reading, ask students to write a business letter that places an order or makes a request or claim.

Suggested Reading:

A Christmas Carol   *Julius Caesar*
Ethan Frome   *Silas Marner*

CHAPTER 11: Writing a Proposal to Solve Problems

Ask students to work in groups to create a new ending for their reading. First, ask students to develop a strategy for creating a new ending. Then, ask them to write a proposal in which they discuss the new ending.

Suggested Reading:

The Call of the Wild   *Lord Jim*
The Grapes of Wrath   *Treasure Island*

CHAPTER 12: Reading and Writing Technical Information

Ask students to choose a character from their reading and assume the character's identity. Then, as the character from the reading, ask them to write a progress report of a situation in which they are involved.

Suggested Reading:

Les Misérables   *The Odyssey*
Moby Dick   *The Scarlet Letter*

CHAPTER 13: Writing and Delivering a Speech

Ask students to choose a character from their reading and assume the character's identity. Tell students to suppose that they will be speaking to a group of students who are interested in the character's career. As the character from the reading, ask students to write a speech that they would give to a group.

Suggested Reading:

Beowulf   *Hamlet*
The Canterbury Tales *The Phantom of the Opera*

CHAPTER 14: Writing and Giving Presentations

Ask students to choose a reading and to suppose that they are travel agents. Ask them to work in pairs to write a persuasive presentation of a vacation destination that will attract visitors. The destination is the setting of their reading. Tell students to provide words or phrases to describe the setting and sensory details to establish a mood.

Suggested Reading:

Gulliver's Travels   *Moby Dick*
Heart of Darkness   *Treasure Island*

These and other titles are available as Adapted Classics from Globe Fearon. For a complete list of Adapted Classics, visit www.globefearon.com.

ANSWER KEY

CHAPTER 1 Your Career Goals

Lesson 1-1 1. Answers should include why an employee expects entry-level skills and explain one skill's importance. **2.** Students should describe how that skill would apply to each situation.

Grammar Workshop 1. SF **2.** SF **3.** SF **4.** S **5.** SF **6.** SF **7.** S **8.** SF **9.** SF **10.** SF. Sentences will vary but should all be complete.

Lesson 1-2 1. Answers should include two positive messages and how they make students feel. **2.** Answers should include why self-confidence is important at school, work, and in private life.

Lesson 1-3 1. Answers will vary depending on the responsibility, but should tell how students practice the habits with their responsibility. **2.** Lists should include descriptions of how the habits could result in better grades.

Lesson 1-4 1. Answers should include three jobs and why they sound interesting to the student. **2.** Answers should tell about a hobby and how it could be useful in a career.

CHAPTER 1 · REVIEW

Key Words 1. self-esteem **2.** economy **3.** mentor **4.** trade-offs **5.** entry-level **6.** assess **7.** attitude **8.** career **9.** career plan **10.** networking

Application: Assess Your Work Skills Answers will vary but should explain students' choices.

Application: Recognize Effective Work Habits 1. Answers should include what Bill has done well in planning his career. **2.** Answers should include three things that the student would tell Bill to solve his problems.

Grammar Workshop Answers will vary but all sentences should be complete.

CHAPTER 2 Finding the Right Job

Lesson 2-1 1. Answers should include three people to use for a job search and the reasons each is appropriate. **2.** Answers should show an understanding of how to stay informed about jobs.

Lesson 2-2 1. A résumé advertises qualities that make you a good worker and positions you as a job hunter. **2.** Answers should include three of the following: work history, school history, work habits, job-related skills, awards, activities, job objective, references.

Lesson 2-3 1. Answers should include three of the following: cover letter applies to specific job, summarizes your skills and how they fit job, is written as a letter, mentions resume is enclosed and that you hope to hear back soon. **2.** Sample answer: can follow directions, has the skills needed, has good work habits.

Lesson 2-3 Grammar Workshop Sample answers: **1.** led **2.** increased **3.** proposed **4.** trained **5.** organized **6.** directed **7.** initiated **8.** supervised **9.** presented **10.** invented

Lesson 2-4 1. Answers should include three of the following: gather interview packet, learn more about the company, rehearse answers to questions, select your interview wardrobe. **2.** Answers should include a summary of the students' qualities and why they should be hired.

Lesson 2-5 1. It can help you improve how you do at later interviews. **2.** A follow-up letter offers thanks for the interview, restates interest in the job, and sums up the skills you bring as a worker.

CHAPTER 2 · REVIEW

Key Words 1. position **2.** flexible **3.** health care **4.** customize **5.** hospitality **6.** retail sales **7.** diplomatic **8.** references **9.** cover letter

Application: Prepare for an Interview 1. Answers should be credible and place the departure in a good light. **2.** Answers will vary, but should show thought on the part of the interviewee. **3.–5.** Answers will vary. Sample answers: **3.** lacks good people skills **4.** will not care about company, or try to be team player **5.** less interested in job than in vacation time

Application: Analyze Job Ads Answers will vary based on the sample ads.

Grammar Workshop Sample answers may include: **1.** Performed; Analyzed; Improved **2.** Answered;

Completed; Resolved; Directed **3.** Reorganized; Compiled; Labeled; Initiated

CHAPTER 3 Being Competent in the Workplace

Lesson 3-1 1. Watch for the behavior a company rewards and learn to practice it. **2.** Answers should show an understanding of teamwork and how it benefits those on a team.

Lesson 3-2 1. A process allows everyone involved to have a say in the decision and to reach better decisions. **2.** Answers should explain decision-making process.

Grammar Workshop Sample answers: **1.** because **2.** ; however, **3.** , and **4.** , but **5.** , and **6.** ; there **7.** , but **8.** , and **9.** ; **10.** , so

Lesson 3-3 1. conflict with a co-worker: focus on the facts, use "I" statements; conflict with a customer: agree if possible and find a way to make the customer happy **2.** A job description explains your responsibilities to avoid conflicts by doing your job and shows what duties are part of your job.

Lesson 3-4 1. Students should choose three of the following: use a calendar, put things in their place, order tasks by importance, estimate work to be done, do work now, do minor tasks regularly. **2.** By being organized, you can control your work, complete tasks, have control over job performance, and gain confidence.

Lesson 3-5 1. Sample answers: self-starter; work well with people, lead, be in charge, be organized, work hard, believe in decisions, persevere, do paperwork on time **2.** Answers should compare buying a franchise and owning a business.

CHAPTER 3 • REVIEW

Key Words 1. alternatives **2.** proactive **3.** entrepreneurs **4.** criteria **5.** prioritize **6.** franchise **7.** probation **8.** company culture **9.** productivity

Application: Analyze Workplace Conflicts Answers should show an understanding of how to identify and resolve workplace conflicts.

Application: Prioritize Tasks 1. Groups should create a task that each member knows something about. **2.** Groups' work should list tasks in order of priority and include a clear explanation of the plan.

Grammar Workshop Sample Answers: **1.** , but **2.** ; however, **3.** ; he **4.** and **5.** , so **6.** , but **7.** years; she **8.** , and **9.** , but **10.** ;

Career File 1. Interviewees should prepare for questions about experience in the field and general work habits. **2.** Résumé should include an interest in science, comfort with technology, and good workplace habits.

UNIT 2 THE PATH TO WRITING SUCCESS

CHAPTER 4 Beginning the Writing Process

Lesson 4-1 1. Steps of the writing process: prewriting, drafting, editing, proofreading, and publishing. **2.** In the manufacturing process the steps follow one another in the same order; the writing process can move back and forth between steps.

Lesson 4-2 1. Answers should show an understanding of the differences among writing to inform, to explain, to describe, and to persuade. **2.** You decide your purpose for writing by deciding your reason for writing and what you are trying to accomplish.

Grammar Workshop Answers will vary but should show an understanding of dependent clauses and phrases.

Lesson 4-3 1. Without limiting a topic to fit the space you have, you will not be able to make all the points you want to make. **2.** Answers should show insight into how purpose will change the report and how the reports will be similar.

Lesson 4-4 1. Answers should explain reasons for using books and magazines, the Internet, and people. **2.** You can judge the accuracy of information by looking at the source, copyright date, publisher of magazine or Web site, obvious bias.

Grammar Workshop 1. contain **2.** are **3.** forget **4.** have **5.** is **6.** are **7.** attend **8.** wants **9.** were **10.** wants

Lesson 4-5 1. Answers should include: chronological order, spatial order, order of importance, cause-and-effect, and comparison and contrast. **2.** In Figure 4-11, every paragraph was best written using a different type of organization.

Grammar Workshop Answers should show an understanding of independent and dependent clauses.

CHAPTER 4 • REVIEW

Key Words 1. a **2.** d **3.** e **4.** g **5.** f **6.** c **7.** h **8.** b

Application: Determining Your Purpose for Writing Sample answers: training programs: explain; an upcoming event: inform; voluntary service: persuade; a store interior: describe.

Application: Narrowing Writing Topics Answers should show understanding how to narrow general topics into specific topics.

Application: Organizing Ideas for Writing 1. cause and effect **2.** comparison and contrast **3.** spatial order **4.** order of importance **5.** spatial order. Students should explain their choices.

Grammar Workshop Part I 1. follows **2.** want **3.** pays **4.** allows **5.** agree **Part II 6.–10.** Answers should show understanding of independent and dependent clauses.

CHAPTER 5 Completing the Writing Process

Lesson 5-1 1. Kendra is writing her travel tips to provide information useful to travelers. **2.** Her letter would have tips for driving, campsites, and would not include information on airlines and hotel reservations.

Grammar Workshop Sample answers: **1.** however **2.** later **3.** In addition **4.** During **5.** however **6.** for example, **7.** Also, **8.** on the other hand **9.** then **10.** such as

Lesson 5-2 1. Students should describe purpose and audience, development and organization, unity and coherence, and word choice. **2.** You can check your work for unity and coherence by looking for a clear topic, clearly presented ideas, a focused presentation, and good transition words.

Grammar Workshop Revisions should make the meaning of the sentences clear.

Lesson 5-3 1. Answers should include two of the following: easily confused words, double negatives, comparative forms, forms of pronouns, double subjects, pronoun referents. **2.** Proofreading is important; the fewer the errors, the better your writing will be received.

Grammar Workshop 1. The Rigby Medical Company, Los Angeles, California **2.** All, Lincoln Memorial **3.** In, Larry, English **4.** Congratulations, Director of Human Resources, Doreen Peterson **5.** Welcome, Mr. Lopez, Our **6.** The, Mount Washington, New Hampshire **7.** I, I **8.** My, Uncle Harry, Yosemite National Park **9.** You, Burnley, Chiropractic Center **10.** One-third, African American, Latino

Lesson 5-4 1. Sample answer: Yes; she provides information travelers can use, the audience is travelers. **2.** A company's printed materials tell how the company sees itself and how professional it is.

CHAPTER 5 · REVIEW

Key Words 1. cliché **2.** informal language **3.** format **4.** draft **5.** unity **6.** graphics **7.** coherence **8.** formal language **9.** diction **10.** inflated diction **11.** copy

Application: Editing a Paragraph 1. b **2.** inform **3.** travelers. Students should explain their answers.

Application: Proofreading a Paragraph How do you tell apart two look-alike bags on an airport baggage carousel? It is easy. You make your bag stand out from everyone else's. Wrap brightly colored electrical tape around the hand of your bag–red, yellow, or lime really stand out. Poisonous insects use bright colors like these so that birds won't eat them. The first thing a person grabs is the handle. If the handle is a bright color, other people will know that it is not their bag. Name tags are hard to read. Initials on the side of the bag are not visible when bags are piled next to each other. A brightly colored handle is your best bet.

Grammar Workshop Sample answers: **Part I 1.** when **2.** In addition **3.** However **4.** Also **5.** such as **Part II 6.–10.** Answers should correct the dangling modifiers **Part III 11.** On Tuesday, Battle of Yorktown. **12.** Senator Jenson, Rugby Motor Company **13.** A, Norway, Europe **14.** The Passaic River, New Jersey. **15.** James, Joanna, Southern Michigan.

Career File 1. Answers should indicate that knowing the audience's likes will help the chef succeed. **2.** This job requires writing, so you would need editing skills; technicians publish records as documents.

UNIT 3 WRITING TO EXPLAIN

CHAPTER 6 Reading and Writing Directions

Lesson 6-1 1. Answers should include three of the following: listen carefully, concentrate on the directions being given, listen to everything, use word clues, ask questions, visualize each step, take notes. **2.** Clue words tell you in which order to do the steps; key words tell you exactly what to do.

Lesson 6-2 1. It is important so you can design directions based on what readers know, their success in the past, and what will motivate them. **2.** do task yourself, have notes for oral presentation, list steps, give directions, ask for comments

Grammar Workshop Answers should show an ability to correct the run-on sentences.

Lesson 6-3 1. You should consider the audience, the importance and length of information, and the speed needed to get the information out. **2.** It creates a professional look, recipients will recognize the memo and know to pay attention.

Grammar Workshop Answers should show an ability to write in the active voice.

CHAPTER 6 • REVIEW

Key Words 1. time clue words **2.** memorandum **3.** brainstorming **4.** e-mail **5.** directions **6.** feedback **7.** Internet

Application: Writing Directions Paragraphs should show a clear progression of steps, with the use of time clue words and phrases to move between directions.

Application: Evaluating Memos and E-mail E-mail: Missing are the TO and SUBJECT lines **Memo:** Missing are the Date and Topic lines

Grammar Workshop Part I 1.–5. Answers should show an ability to correct run-on sentences. **Part II 6.–10.** Answers should be in the active voice.

CHAPTER 7 Writing to Explain a Process

Lesson 7-1 1. Students should describe preview, read, write, and review. **2.** Answers should show evidence that students understand the four steps.

Lesson 7-2 1. The explanation should cover what is important for the purpose and should be understood by the audience. **2.** Answers should show an understanding of the sources students would use.

Lesson 7-3 1. For a general audience, you would write an overview; for an expert audience, you would give a more detailed explanation. **2.** Students should explain clarity, completeness, and organization.

Grammar Workshop 1. Jane and Rita their. **2.** salespeople their **3.** man his **4.** plants their **5.** Ann her **6.** woman she **7.** workers their **8.** shop its **9.** Your you **10.** I my

Lesson 7-4 1. Precise details make it easier for readers to form a picture of the process. **2.** Denotation is exact meaning; connotation is the feeling connected to a word. Accept reasonable samples.

Lesson 7-5 1. Graphics provide a visual way to understand a process. **2.** Tables present statistics so that they are easy to understand and interpret; line graphs compare one piece of information with another.

Grammar Workshop Answers show relevant sections. **1.** Wendy, my business partner, graduated **2.** chorus, changing costumes, and **3.** Simone, it's **4.** Willy, George, and Lizzie **5.** billing, Ms. Wylie? **6.** program, which . . . idea, takes **7.** Order staples, printer paper, and memo **8.** dogs, cats, birds, and **9.** hurry, Keisha, or **10.** Inez, the most.

CHAPTER 7 • REVIEW

Key Words 1. b **2.** h **3.** e **4.** f **5.** d **6.** c **7.** g **8.** a

Application: Explain a Process to Two Audiences Students' writing should include the correct steps in order, and written for two different audiences.

Application: Sort and Organize Information A: Prepare pulp, remove dirt, turn pulp into paper, cut paper **B.** Heat the coals, place the steak on a rack, turn the steak over, remove cooked steak **C.** Choose topic, research topic, take notes, organize notes, write draft, edit draft, publish.

Grammar Workshop Part I 1. her **2.** them **3.** her **4.** their **5.** they **Part II 6.** My brother, a cat lover, got a job at an animal shelter. **7.** On the morning of March 1, the company moved to a new building. **8.** Correct. **9.** Waving her arms, the crossing guard stopped the children from crossing. **10.** Correct.

Career File 1. Being a cashier involves processes such as running the register and dealing with money, and would communicate through talking and memos. **2.** Restaurant managers may gather information through technical manuals, personal knowledge, and interviews.

CHAPTER 8 Writing Reports That Describe

Lesson 8-1 1. Similarities: both have information the business needs; differences: informal reports are short, with little research; formal reports need planning, research, organizing. **2.** An incident report is necessary when something unusual happens in the workplace.

Grammar Workshop 1. among **2.** accept **3.** less **4.** Except **5.** well **6.** fewer **7.** well **8.** effect **9.** between **10.** affect

Lesson 8-2 1. Students should list the following: learn about the interviewee, write questions, set up the interview, conduct the interview, thank your interview subject, ask if you can call back to confirm quotes. **2.** Possible answer: primary source: when using quotations; secondary source: when using someone's analysis

Lesson 8-3 1. Students should describe: introduction, body, and conclusion. **2.** Comparison-and-contrast order: contrast each major point, or complete the argument for one side, then the other; order of importance: points organized from least to most, or most to least important.

Grammar Workshop Relevant sections: **1.** displayed, sold, and serviced **2.** listen, learn, and ask **3.** football, baseball, and hockey **4.** sells popcorn, ushers people to their seats, and runs **5.** doesn't work and disappoints **6.** paid her parking fine, ate lunch, and ran **7.** calling on customers, explaining products, and giving service **8.** Studying to be a doctor and practicing **9.** buy our products, use our services, and need our company **10.** Singing, dancing, and fencing

Lesson 8-4 1. An outline helps you to see how your main points and details relate and what information you need to gather. **2.** Students should list the steps for outlining shown on page 158.

Grammar Workshop 1. their **2.** its **3.** its **4.** cut **5.** stands **6.** their **7.** its **8.** has **9.** is **10.** practices

Lesson 8-5 1. Students should list and describe three of the following: facts, statistics, quotations, definitions, anecdotes, examples, reasons, and comparisons. **2.** Supporting details help readers understand your ideas.

Lesson 8-6 1. Footnotes should include the author of the information and the place from which it came. **2.** Students should list the following: do not use slang, avoid contractions, stick to the point, avoid using exclamation points, use formal titles to refer to people.

Grammar Workshop Answers should contain no redundancies.

CHAPTER 8 · REVIEW

Key Words 1. executive summary **2.** font **3.** search engine **4.** informal report **5.** database **6.** secondary source **7.** concise **8.** formal report **9.** synopsis **10.** thesis statement **11.** primary source **12.** keyword search **13.** relevant

Application: Create an Outline Student outlines should be well-organized and use outline style.

Application: Finding Sources and Organizing a Report Preparation should show that students understand finding sources and report organization.

Grammar Workshop Part I 1. well **2.** among **3.** fewer **4.** accept **5.** effect **Part II.** Relevant sections: **6.** Sorting, stamping, and delivering **7.** cared for patients and gave them **8.** a pencil, a notepad, and a sample **9.** Writing a draft, revising it, and producing **10.** Wherever you go, whatever you do, whomever you happen to visit **Part III 11.** marches **12.** their **13.** their **14.** produces **15.** wants **Part IV 16.–20.** Answers should contain no redundancies.

CHAPTER 9 Writing to Persuade

Lesson 9-1 1. Student answers should show an understanding of what persuasive writing is. **2.** preview to predict what you will read, read, then take notes, review what you have learned

Lesson 9-2 1. You should consider your purpose and audience so that your readers will understand the action you want them to take. **2.** People feel emotion about pets, and appealing to emotion can be a powerful technique.

Grammar Workshop Sample relevant sections: **1.** hard, but **2.** because **3.** floor and I'll **4.** report because he **5.** José after he **6.** park after all **7.** skills because the **8.** pets and for **9.** Both Juan and Adela **10.** Neither Donna nor Terry

Lesson 9-3 1. Graphics can help a reader see your ideas and persuade them visually. **2.** You would use a bar graph, because it compares information.

Lesson 9-4 1. The writer gave reasons, wrote about benefits, made an offer to the "most loyal customers," made a call to action, offered an extra reason to call. **2.** Personal appeal: audience is a person; mass mailings: large audience; direct mailing: audience is specific group.

Grammar Workshop 1. than **2.** Its **3.** They're **4.** to, there **5.** then **6.** their **7.** too **8.** two **9.** its **10.** It's, their

Lesson 9-5 1. Answers should show that students understand similarities and differences between ads and catalog copy. **2.** Student answers should show an understanding of the principles of writing ads.

Grammar Workshop 1. borrowed **2.** will move **3.** sells **4.** changed **5.** likes **6.** will tow **7.** stopped, walked **8.** needs **9.** helped **10.** smiled

Lesson 9-6 1. Students should list and give an example for: who, what, where, when, why **2.** Answer should explain the differences between a press release and an ad.

CHAPTER 9 • REVIEW

Key Words 1. direct mailing **2.** media **3.** testimonials **4.** tone **5.** data chart **6.** mass mailing **7.** press release **8.** bar graph **9.** pictographs **10.** hook

Application: Techniques of Persuasive Writing 1. testimonial **2.** self-interest **3.** fact **4.** emotion **5.** emotion. Students should explain their choices.

Application: Choose a Type of Persuasive Writing 1. press release **2.** sales letter **3.** ad **4.** direct mailing; Students should explain their choices.

Grammar Workshop Relevant parts of sample answers: **Part I 1.–5.:1.** , and **2.** , but **3.** ; **4.** because **5.** , and **Part II 6.** It's **7.** there **8.** than **9.** to **10.** its **Part III 11.** will finish **12.** worked **13.** stopped, let **14.** will explain **15.** will describe

Career File 1. Data-entry clerks would need to organize information in an office, such as files and billing. **2.** Paralegals might do persuasive writing connected with persuading clients and making arguments in court.

UNIT 5 WRITING IN BUSINESS

CHAPTER 10 Writing Business Letters

Lesson 10-1 1. Students should list the following: to request, to inform, to persuade. **2.** The purpose of the letter is to inform; it tells how a company plans to resolve a problem.

Lesson 10-2 1. Similarity: both are people who pay a company; differences: clients pay for a service, customers buy a product. **2.** A marketing plan can help find new clients and customers for businesses that need them.

Grammar Workshop 1. chose **2.** drove **3.** flew **4.** has begun **5.** broke **6.** are grown **7.** has ridden **8.** brought **9.** ran **10.** written

Lesson 10-3 1. Your letter should use language and tone addressed to that audience and purpose. **2.** Order letter: straightforward, includes details to help you get what you order; request letter: friendlier, written to ask someone to do something.

Lesson 10-4 1. Students should list and describe the following: block style, modified-block style, indented style. **2.** Date on right, paragraphs indented and separated by lines, close and signature on the right, left margin flush, right not flush

Lesson 10-5 1. People respond better to positive language. **2.** A business letter can stress the company's willingness to serve, tell benefits of dealing with the company, address concerns, and tell how the company can meet them.

Grammar Workshop 1. counsel **2.** personal **3.** stationery **4.** personnel **5.** stationery **6.** principles **7.** personnel **8.** council **9.** principle **10.** stationary

Lesson 10-6 1. A writer should edit for content and organization, as well as make sure the message, purpose, audience, and tone are correct. **2.** A peer editor can catch problems and errors you may have missed.

CHAPTER 10 • REVIEW

Key Words 1. return address **2.** indented-style letter **3.** modified-block style **4.** salutation **5.** marketing plan **6.** claim letter **7.** empathy **8.** block-style letter **9.** marketing **10.** adjustment letter

Application: Reading and Analyzing a Business Letter 1. request letter **2.** block style **3.** The purpose is to solicit donations. **4.** The audience is public TV viewers. **5.** The writer hopes the reader will send money.

Application: Revising Business Letters Revisions should show clear language and appropriate tone.

Grammar Workshop Part I 1. Correct. **2.** caught **3.** did **4.** was thrown **5.** saw **Part II 6.** principal **7.** personnel **8.** stationery **9.** council **10.** principal

CHAPTER 11 Writing a Proposal to Solve Problems

Lesson 11-1 1. A proposal is a formal, written plan for an action to improve a situation or solve a problem. **2.** An RFP asks people to submit proposals to solve a problem.

Lesson 11-2 1. If you understand the customer's needs, you can customize the RFP to suit those needs. **2.** Brainstorming can help you think through the problem and determine the cost of the job.

Grammar Workshop Relevant sections of answers: **1.** "I . . . work," **2.** "Read . . ., called 'How . . . Ahead.' " **3.** "It . . . work," said. **4.** is, "Sarks . . . smile." **5.** "Tonight's . . . sauce," **6.** "Prices . . . . Tomorrow" **7.** "Safety First" is **8.** "I must agree," "The . . . moved." **9.** "Beware . . . Dogs," **10.** "We . . . accounting,"

Lesson 11-3 1. A strategy focuses on how best to solve the problem or meet the need. **2.** You may find that other solutions are better than the first one proposed.

Lesson 11-4 1. Supporting information shows the writer has done the research and helps persuade readers with specifics. **2.** You could find the information in a survey or in magazine and newspaper articles.

Grammar Workshop Answers should show understanding of how to use appropriate language.

Lesson 11-5 1. The writing process helps you organize and revise your work so your proposal presents a strong case. **2.** Sample answer: Yes, because she has made a strong case with details that support her proposal.

Grammar Workshop 1. 555-6101 **2.** six **3.** 1976 **4.** $1 billion **5.** 5:15 **6.** $310 **7.** 22 percent **8.** Seven, 7, 2001 **9.** 3, 29616 **10.** 8:30

Lesson 11-6 1. Students should list three of the following: change type, change font, add color, add photographs, graphs, tables, or charts. **2.** Visuals can help a reader understand and see information in a new way.

CHAPTER 11 · REVIEW

Key Words 1. quote **2.** appendix **3.** vendors **4.** proposal **5.** RFP **6.** focus group **7.** clip-art **8.** strategy statement **9.** documentation

Application: Analyzing a Problem and Developing a Strategy Students' proposals should show an understanding of how to write a proposal and strategy statement.

Application: Reading and Analyzing an RFP 1. refrigerators **2.** $55,000, three months **3.** client list, history, experience with grocery stores **4.** January 12

Grammar Workshop Part I 1. "Never," he said, "I'd rather quit." **2.** "Did you read the article 'Save Now or Else' in today's paper?" **3.** Mammoth Marsh-mallow's slogan read, "Soft as an Angel's Wing." **4.** "You shouted 'Stop!' " said the train engineer, "so I pulled the brake." **5.** "You break it, you buy it," says the sign at Ultra Antiques. **Part II** Sample answers for **6.–10**: **6.** You can leave, and I'll follow when I can. **7.** The proposal to have music in the cafeteria was exciting. **8.** Can you please take this memo to the president? **9.** "I'd love the opportunity to work for you." **10.** Is that necessary now? **Part III 11.** One **12.** 80 **13.** 100 **14.** 200 **15.** Two thousand

CHAPTER 12 Reading and Writing Technical Information

Lesson 12-1 1. Technical writing explains how a product or process works. **2.** Answers should explain differences and similarities between technical articles and reports.

Grammar Workshop 1. strong **2.** most interesting **3.** cheaper **4.** more colorful **5.** fastest **6.** hardest **7.** clearer **8.** happier **9.** longer **10.** sharper

Lesson 12-2 1. Answer should explain differences between writing for a general audience and for specialists. **2.** Students should list and explain the following: parts to whole order, chronological order, spatial order, chronological order.

Lesson 12-3 1. A lab report presents the results of experiments and helps people learn from the experiences of others. **2.** Graphics can be used to show data, results, and information more clearly than words.

Grammar Workshop 1. Does **2.** donate **3.** start **4.** work **5.** tries **6.** takes **7.** wait **8.** practice **9.** want, hope **10.** keeps

Lesson 12-4 1. A school report shows the educational progress of a student. **2.** Progress reports focus on the status of a project, including how much has been completed and when the rest will be done.

Grammar Workshop 1. eighty-five **2.** two-thirds, one-third **3.** old-fashioned **4.** all-time **5.** twenty-one **6.** sister-in-law **7.** half-time **8.** three-fourths, twenty-four **9.** great-grandmother **10.** thirty-three

Lesson 12-5 1. A manual has instructions for installing, using, or repairing a product for users. **2.** They can tell you if your instructions make sense so you can edit them.

Lesson 12-6 1. Students should list the following: photographs, diagrams, tables, bar graphs, pie charts, line graphs, highlighted areas. **2.** Sample answer: No, because you would need words to help explain the visuals and what was in the book.

CHAPTER 12 · REVIEW

Key Words 1. liability **2.** trade journals **3.** technical writing **4.** E-commerce **5.** objective **6.** manual **7.** bias **8.** logo **9.** prototype **10.** align

Application: Read and Evaluate Technical Writing Answers should show understanding of technical writing.

Application: Create a Lab Report Answers should show understanding of the procedures of a lab report.

Grammar Workshop Part I 1. greater **2.** most beautiful **3.** more quickly **4.** simpler **5.** better **Part II 6.** tells **7.** want **8.** stay **9.** has **10.** bothers **Part III 11.** first-rate **12.** thirty-four **13.** ex-postal **14.** above-average, year-end **15.** half-brother, all-pro

Career File 1. Answers should show an understanding that managers would write different types of reports. **2.** Answers should show an understanding that these jobs require reading and writing a variety of reports.

UNIT 6 SPEECHES AND PRESENTATIONS

CHAPTER 13 Writing and Delivering a Speech

Lesson 13-1 1. It may have too much information and confuse an audience. **2.** Answers should explain two ways of narrowing a topic, with examples of each.

Lesson 13-2 1. Students should list and give examples for each of the following: persuade, inform, entertain. **2.** Most speeches inform workers about work-related issues.

Lesson 13-3 1. Students should list the following: chronological, topical, problem-solution order. **2.** Listeners can better follow and understand information that is organized.

Grammar Workshop 1. On Monday, of towels that she put on the display cases **2.** down Maple, across Main, over to Hampton **3.** on the Great Lakes in Ohio **4.** on the rack beside the door **5.** Except for Sarah, from Temp-O Services **6.** from this office to the cafeteria for lunch **7.** out of business **8.** with Hector and Rosa, at the hospital **9.** for degrees in their careers **10.** with slides

Lesson 13-4 1. Accept answers that summarize how to give a speech. **2.** Answers should list five tips.

Lesson 13-5 1. Active listening is paying attention and responding; passive listening is uninvolved. **2.** Students should list the following: know why you are listening, pay attention, keep an open mind, think about what you already know.

Grammar Workshop 1. Dear Dr. Thorne: **2.** following products: apples **3.** qualities: skill **4.** 5:00 **5.** said: "Hard **6.** Concern: **7.** hour: Route 5 **8.** salesperson: fairness **9.** sections: past sales **10.** customer: "If

CHAPTER 13 · REVIEW

Key Words 1. manuscript **2.** eye contact **3.** monotone **4.** active listening **5.** guide phrases **6.** impromptu **7.** passive listening **8.** statistics **9.** podium **10.** body language

Application: Organize a Speech 1. chronological **2.** problem-solution **3.** problem-solution **4.** chronological **5.** topical. Students should explain their choices.

Application: Define the Purpose of a Speech 1. persuade **2.** entertain **3.** inform **4.** inform **5.** persuade. Students should explain their answers.

Grammar Workshop Part I 1. Besides changing the oil, of the cars, from the dealership. **2.** between Ray and Sally, from Enrique. **3.** by noon, for them **4.** to meet, with Shanice and Leanne **5.** between nine and six **Part II 6.** following: a stapler **7.** President: **8.** 8:30, 10:00 **9.** 10:15 **10.** foods: salad

CHAPTER 14 Writing and Giving Presentations

Lesson 14-1 1. Summary should show an understanding of how to use visual aids. **2.** Answers should give advantages of each method being used in a presentation.

Lesson 14-2 1. A speaker should prepare for a speech by practicing; a presentation by practice and also making sure the equipment works. **2.** Sample answer: when you need to show pictures, numbers, and reinforce points

Grammar Workshop 1. attorneys-at-law **2.** mice **3.** knives **4.** spoonsful **5.** boxes, watches **6.** businesses **7.** bagsful, groceries **8.** feet, feet **9.** companies, women, children **10.** secretaries, duties

Lesson 14-2 1. Handouts remind listeners of the main points of the presentation, persuade and/or sell, entertain the audience **2.** Sample answer: handouts that inform about safety, persuade to use equipment, persuade to buy safety equipment

Lesson 14-3 1. Students should list the following: practice, practice in front of friends, arrive early and test visual aids, find out about the mood of the audience, practice in the room if possible **2.** You could use extra visuals, anecdotes, or interesting stories.

Grammar Workshop 1. Which report should I finish first? **2.** Angela, show Chuck how to add toner to the printer. **3.** Dr. and Mrs. Graham Jackson started the business in 1976. **4.** The marketing department says that it's time to send out the brochures. **5.** Winn carves tables and chairs for Greene's Department Store. **6.** "I'll never finish," said the secretary, looking at the pile of work. **7.** The Lupes and the Fletches are skilled carpenters. **8.** Vanessa, head of the company blood drive, works in my department. **9.** Ms. Bingley said, "We'll choose the photos tomorrow." **10.** Bateman's stores have announced their new sale prices.

Lesson 14-5 1. A meeting leader should decide if the meeting is necessary, invite necessary attendees, set an agenda, arrange a meeting place, run the meeting. **2.** Answers should explain the responsibilities of both leader and participant.

CHAPTER 14 · REVIEW

Key Words 1. flip chart **2.** overhead projector **3.** storyboard **4.** landscape **5.** agenda **6.** visual aids **7.** parliamentary procedure **8.** template **9.** transparencies **10.** portrait

Application: Organize a Presentation Steps should show an understanding of how to give a presentation.

Application: Analyze Presentation Handouts Student answers should show understanding how to improve presentation skills.

Grammar Workshop Part I 1. children **2.** Men and women **3.** loaves **4.** companies, discoveries **5.** brothers-in-law **Part II 6.** "Why is Sharon late for the meeting?" asked Janice. **7.** The correct closing for a business letter is "Yours sincerely." **8.** A proposal is what you write when you have an idea to solve a problem. **9.** "I never missed a deadline," said Mrs. Martinez. **10.** Mr. Covello said, "Your presentation was very informative, Joanna."

Career File 1. Answers should describe how to organize a speech to give to high schoolers. **2.** Accept answers that list tips and show an understanding of presentations.